Yukari Shirota and Tosiyasu L. Kunii

First Book on UNIX™
for Executives

Springer-Verlag
Tokyo Berlin Heidelberg New York
1984

Dedicated to Hideko S. Kunii and
to the memory of Mr. Kazue Ishii

Yukari Shirota

Research Staff of
Kunii Laboratory of Computer Science
Department of Information Science
Faculty of Science
The University of Tokyo

Prof. Dr. Tosiyasu L. Kunii

Department of Information Science
Faculty of Science
The University of Tokyo

ISBN-13: 978-4-431-70003-6   e-ISBN-13: 978-4-431-68023-9
DOI: 10.1007/978-4-431-68023-9

Library of Congress Card No.: 84-23638

Preface

A good introduction to a new product or concept is vital. This is particularly true for a versatile software system such as UNIX. UNIX provides the depth and intelligence to make your computer work hard for you. It will help you create software and help you use your office automation equipment to create and edit documents. For your introduction to UNIX, you want a great little book. That is what this work is meant to be. This book is designed for non-computer specialists, especially for executives, administrators and managers who want to make better use of their software specialists and experts.

The way this Springer edition has come to be published is itself a story. Back about 1980, the founder and president of one of the more successful microcomputer companies, Mr. Kazue Ishii of CEC, wanted to start somethig that would be brilliant, sophisticated, innovative, and which would grow steadily. Out of many proposals, the one he accepted happened to be mine. The proposal was to build a family of network workstations for computer-aided design/manufacturing and office automation. UNIX was to be used as a software generator. But he had a hard time understanding UNIX, what good it is and how good it is...

Spending a significant amount of time with a popular computer columnist, Miss Yukari Shirota, I compiled this book for him. I found this book generally useful for top executives, managers, planners and office administrators whose background is outside software engineering. Dr. Heinz Götze, President of Springer-Verlag, liked this book personally, and decided to publish the Springer edition. Dr. Harold Solomon, a geophysical fluid dynamicist, translated the original Techno Japanese edition into English. Dr. Lou Katz, President of USENIX Association, which is one of the largest UNIX professional societies in the world, reviewed the translation with me. The result is now in your hands to guide you through the wonderland of UNIX.

I hope that you will enjoy this book, and that you will try out UNIX the first chance you get.

Tosiyasu L. Kunii

UNIX is a trademark of AT&T Bell Laboratories.

Contents

Chapter 4   Characteristic Features of UNIX

Chapter 1
Why UNIX, Now?

Popularity of UNIX

UNIX was developed by Ken Thompson, Dennis Ritchie and coworkers at Bell Telephone Laboratories in 1969. The initial version was created on the Digital Equipment Corporation (DEC) PDP-7 minicomputer.

UNIX is an operating system, a supervisory program that makes it more efficient for you to make the computer work.

Thompson originally had a personal reason for developing UNIX. At the time he developed the package, all of the existing operating systems were difficult to use, and he wanted one for his own use that would create a more comfortable programming environment.

UNIX became a very good operating system; therefore, other people also used it. The number of users within Bell Laboratories gradually increased; many of them added their own improvements, making it an even better operating system. As many people added improvements to UNIX, the amount of software that it can supervise (for simplicity we will refer to it as software which operates on UNIX) steadily increased.

The first use of UNIX outside Bell Laboratories was on the PDP-11 series of minicomputers produced by DEC. UNIX was gradually adapted for use on other computers

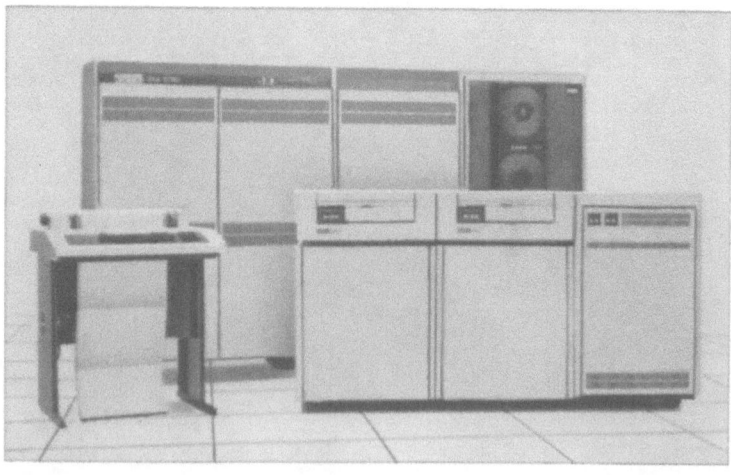

The VAX-11/780 super mini-computer made by DEC. UNIX runs on the VAX series

A computer of the CEC8000 SUPERBASE series in an office

besides the DEC PDP-11 series. It now operates on the Amdahl VM/370, the BBN Computer C Machine, the Perkin-Elmer Interdata 8/32, the IBM 360/370 series, and the VAX series "super minicomputers", which are high class versions of the PDP-11.

Since the UNIX operating system is very easy to use, its design concept had a great influence on operating systems for microcomputers. Examples of UNIX-based microcomputer operating systems are the OS-9 system which Microware Systems developed for use on the 6809 8-bit CPU, the Decision-I Z80 system, produced by Morrow designs, and Cromix, which runs on the Z80 8-bit CPU of the Cromemco microcomputer system. To be sure, running UNIX on an 8-bit CPU does increase the load on the CPU, but there are a number of microcomputers which have a UNIX-like operating system running on an 8-bit CPU. As more and more microcomputers utilize a 16-bit rather than an 8-bit CPU, the attitude toward the operating system is becoming **"UNIX, of course!"** Advertisements for 16-bit CPUs like the 8086, the Z8000 and the 68000 almost invariably boast about their adoption of UNIX.

Some microcomputers developed in Japan also use UNIX. One example is the Chuo Electronics Company's CEC8000, which uses the Z8000 CPU. In America, software companies such as Microsoft, Interactive and UniSoft supply UNIX-like operating systems. Machines on which UNIX runs include the Onyx C8002 (with a

UNIX is used as an operating system on many computers, from large main frame computers down to mini-computers and microcomputers

Z8000 CPU), the Zilog System 8000 (also with a Z8000 CPU) and many others.

Recently, UNIX has been used as the operating system on a number of personal computers, including the IBM-PC and the Apple "Lisa". These computers are certain to increase the number of UNIX fans. The UCB (University of California, Berkeley) version 4.2 BSD runs on the Sun Microsystem Sun Workstation (with 68000 CPUs). UNIX is also used on the Hewlett-Packard HP-9000 (with 32-bit CPUs). Among UNIX-like systems, IDRIS supported by Whitesmiths is widely used, and the Apollo Domain 32-bit super minicomputer (with 68000 CPUs), produced by Apollo has been greatly influenced by UNIX.

When an operating system is used by so many people and machines, then its system brings several advantages to the user. One distinct advantage is that, even if computer hardware differs, when they run the same operating system then the computers can be operated in the same way. Therefore, once you learn to use one computer, you know how to use many different computers. Many programs are available for a standard operating system. Therefore, it is of interest for the user to know which operating system will be the most widely used.

The same commands can be used on computers made by any company as long as the operating system is UNIX

UNIX is now very widely used on a great variety of computers, from main frame computers such as the IBM 370 series to microcomputers. UNIX's popularity does not depend on the size of the computer. The dissemination of this system, which was originally used only inside of Bell Laboratories, to a wide range of users is testimony that it is a superior, easy-to-use operating system.

In America, most computer companies are already using and selling UNIX and UNIX-like operating systems. It is widely used in office automation. One of the top office automation companies in the U.S.A., Interactive Systems, has created an office automation software system based on UNIX, called IS/1, and it has become a bestseller. Almost all computer science departments in universities use UNIX in education and research. There is no doubt that the popularity of UNIX as an operating system will continue to increase in the future.

What is UNIX?

UNIX is an operating system, in other words, a program that supervises a computer

The concept of an **operating system** (abbreviated OS) is a difficult one to explain. In essence, an operating system is a program which supervises a computer, and which is necessary to make the computer run efficiently enough to be of practical use. The actual computer machinery (the "hardware") and the programs used in individual applications (the "applications software") are not enough in themselves to make the computer run easily. In order for an instruction to be transmitted to the computer and for the computer to carry out that instruction well, a program which supervises the computer is also needed. A good analogy is a company or government department in which it is not enough to have only the people who do the actual work; administrators to run the organization are also needed.

There are different types of operating systems for different purposes and computer systems.

UNIX has the following characteristics:

1. It is global.
2. It is aimed at multiple users.
3. It is interactive.
4. It is time sharing.
5. It is multi-programming.

Global

Program
development is
easy

UNIX has a
word processing
capability

UNIX can be
used for office
automation

Writing
mathematical papers
is easy

Since UNIX is a general-
purpose operating system, it
can be used to do many
different kinds of jobs

Let us now examine what these terms mean.

1. A **global** operating system is not intended only for
one specialized use, but can be used in many different
applications. On one occasion it might be used for office
automation, on another occasion for controlling experimental apparatus, and on still another occasion for
developing new programs.

2. A **multi-user** system permits a number of different
users to use the computer at the same time. UNIX
permits a number of terminals to be connected to one
computer. Each user has exclusive use of one terminal,
from which he or she gives the computer instructions.
When a user inputs an instruction from a terminal, an
answer comes back from the computer immediately.

3. An **interactive** system permits a "conversation" between the user and the CPU. This interaction may be
displayed on a CRT (cathode ray tube, which is similar to
a television screen), or it may be printed out on paper by a
teletype-like printer.

4. **Time sharing** means that when two or more jobs
are done on the computer at the same time, a small
amount of CPU time is given to each job in succession.

The computer does only a little of each job at a time. The operating system has to keep track of how far along each job is and start the work from that point when the job's turn comes up. The rate at which a human being can feed input into a computer is very slow compared to the rate at which the computer can process it. In the time it takes the human to get his input typed in, the computer can do other work and then get back to him. This means that any one user does not have to worry about being made to wait very long, and it eliminates the waste of CPU time that would occur without time sharing. **Time sharing system** is sometimes abbreviated to TSS.

5. **Multi-programming** concept is based on user's jobs and computer tasks. From the viewpoint of a computer (strictly speaking, a CPU), a task is a work unit. From a user's viewpoint, a work unit is a job (program) or a command. One job consists of one task or several tasks, and one task may invoke other tasks in turn. A word "process" is used in the same sense as a task. A multi-programming (or multi-job) system permits a single user to run several programs (jobs) at the same time. A user can create another job before he completes the previous job.

Interactive

The user works by talking to the computer through a terminal

Time-sharing

UNIX divides CPU time up into very short segments and does each job a little bit at a time. This is called time-sharing

Applications of UNIX

UNIX, being a global operating system, has many applications. A **programmer** (a person who creates computer programs) can use UNIX as a program development system. UNIX provides many tools for program development. The **editor**, for example, is used to type in a program from a keyboard. It is an important factor in computer use. If the editor is not used properly, the efficiency of the work falls off considerably. And in UNIX there are many processing systems for the computer language (such as COBOL, FORTRAN, Pascal, C, etc.). Other tools, such as debuggers and a compiler-compiler, are also available to help make it easier to create programs.

The UNIX system can be applied to office automation. UNIX has the capability to act as a powerful **word processor**. Letters, documents, etc. can be created easily and then stored in memory. Modifications are easy to make. The documents can be arranged in any desired format and then sent, as pretty format text, to any recipient, such as a printer or phototypesetter.

A format package for algebraic formulas that is convenient for preparing papers in the physical sciences and engineering is also available. Complicated expressions such as

$$\sum_{m=1}^{N} \frac{e^{-Am}}{1 - e^{-Ax}} \{\sin(\pi m x) + m \cos(\pi m x)\}^2$$

can be handled right along with regular text.

There are also many special programs, for use in preparing format texts of documents, detecting spelling mistakes, etc.

UNIX makes it possible for users to communicate through electronic mail. When the user starts to interact with the computer terminal, the computer first informs him whether any letters have arrived. He can then read the mail and save or discard it. Electronic mail is very convenient as a means of communication between frequent computer users. Since the same letter can be

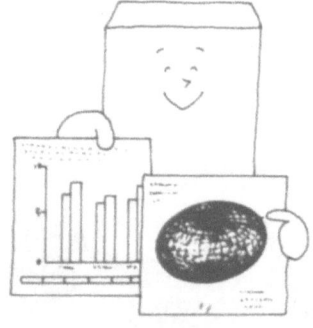

If you connect the main computer to hardware that has a graphic capability, you can produce beautiful computer graphics

UNIX provides many tools for program development

addressed to a number of different people, the user can distribute by a single operation project progress reports, internal company reports, notices of meetings, invitations to picnics or parties, etc.

Also a user can communicate with another user through a terminal. His message is sent to the other's terminal display as soon as he inputs something. If the recipient of the message is using the computer, the message will interrupt his work to tell him he has a message. When the recipient is not using the computer or is busy with other work, the message is stored in the computer for retrieval at any time.

UNIX offers a data base capability. Information that has been input is stored as a data base. The necessary instructions are available to search for, retrieve, and process information in the data base. UNIX also offers the capability of preparing whatever graphics the hardware is capable of. Charts and graphs of experimental results and business achievements have greater visual impact and make it easier to conceptualize the information than do data not represented in graphic form.

UNIX is well-suited for computer control of experimental equipment and factory machinery, because it makes connections to other devices relatively easy through user defined device drivers.

Finally, the UNIX system includes game programs.

Characteristics of UNIX

The original concept of UNIX was that of an operating system that would enable the individual user to do whatever he wants with the computer. UNIX's first priority is given to the efficiency of programming. Compared to many previous operating systems, which had the efficient use of hardware as their main objective, UNIX's main objective is to increase the efficiency of the person doing the programming. However, as UNIX is further

developed, a number of improvements will be made
which will also permit hardware to be used more
efficiently. For example, as the block size can be adjusted
to the user's application programs, a disc access gets
better.

A **command** is an instructional word that is used in the
man-machine interaction. Commands are different for
each operating system; a person using an operating system for the first time must therefore learn its unique
commands. The UNIX command system is simple. Once
learned, it is fun to use. However, messages from the
computer to the programmer are few, being limited
mainly to messages that are put out when the programmer
makes an error. This characteristic aims UNIX at the
advanced programmer rather than the beginner. For an
advanced programmer, programming is easier without
receiving numerous messages, but the beginner might
feel uneasy about what he just did.

UNIX, being a superior program development system,
makes it easy to develop programs which run on it. Since
UNIX users include the computer science departments of
universities and leading company industrial programmers,
including, of course, those at Bell Laboratories, there has
been a steady accumulation of high-quality software developed with UNIX.

UNIX also makes it easy for one programmer to use
programs that were developed by another. Previously, it
was rare for a programmer to use a program developed by
another; more commonly each programmer wrote his
own program, even though the content of the programs
was basically the same. This led to much wasted effort.
Without specific instructions, it was difficult to use someone else's program. UNIX permits one user to use
programs which others write. A good example is game
programs such as chess and rogue. Also, users can add
their custom-made commands to UNIX commands easily.
This can be done simply by placing the file containing the
user defined commands at a common area. These programs are regarded as common property and are widely
used.

However, there are occasionally some programs or data

What is UNIX?

which one doesn't want others to see, to use, or to change. UNIX has a protective capability for use in such circumstances; the creator of a program can put restrictions on it. He can prohibit use, readout, and writing in (alterations and deletions); permission for each of these can be restricted to only the owner, or to a specified group. For example, if several people form a project team and create a secret program, permission to have access to the program can be limited to only that group.

When a user works with UNIX, he rarely does all of the necessary programming himself. UNIX provides a number of convenient software tools, and it is sometimes sufficient to combine them. (In fact this was done a number of times in the actual development of UNIX.) Two or more previously developed tools combine to form a more complicated tool; similarly, a number of existing commands combine to form a more specialized command for one's own use.

Commands are easily combined in UNIX, because the entrances and exits of most commands in UNIX (properly called the standard input and standard output, respectively) are perfectly matched. Therefore, in UNIX, one need not worry about the problem encountered so often with other operating systems: that, when two programs are connected (making one program's output another's input), the difference in standards used in the connecting parts forces the programmer to spend many hours trying to match them up. The connectors are uniform, so the connections are easy to make. (For further details on this subject, refer to the explanation of "Data Flow and Pipes" in Chapter 4.)

One of the main reasons for the popularity of UNIX is its freedom. Since the source program of UNIX is written in a high level language, and is available by paying a fee, a programmer who is really interested can study it and make improvements to suit his taste. This is a great boon for programmers who are dissatisfied with the specifications of commercially available operating systems. Most universities have purchased the source program. A good example of such a modified system is the UCB version of UNIX. Of course, not all programmers wish to develop

Multi-user

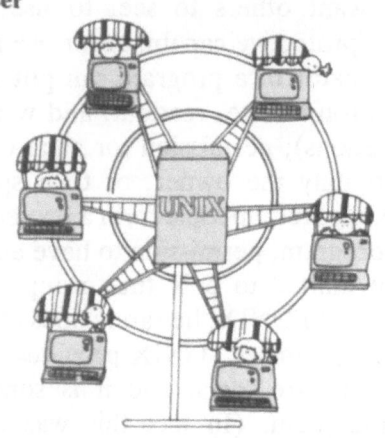

A multi-user system can be used by a number of people at once. This means that a number of terminals are connected to one central computer

Multi-programming

One user can do a number of jobs (programs) on UNIX at one time, so it is called a multi-programming system

whole new versions; one might simply not like one particular command. A new command that a programmer makes up can be distributed so that it becomes available to all UNIX users. This kind of modification is very easy with UNIX; the system is therefore steadily evolving. Some people complain that this makes the naming of UNIX commands inconsistent, and therefore hard to learn. Also the abbreviations (for example, list is **ls**) differ widely from the conventions that are used in other popular operating systems. However, a user can always rename a command to his own favorite one.

Since UNIX is a **multi-user** operating system, it can be used by a number of people at the same time, provided that a number of terminals are connected to one computer. The greatest advantage is obtained from UNIX in an office, research laboratory or business where a number of people are using the computer.

UNIX also permits one user to run a number of jobs at one time. This is called **multi-programming**. A job which is visible to the user (keyed-in data is input to that job), is called a **foreground job** in UNIX. And the other jobs which are independent of a terminal and run behind the scenes are called **background jobs**. The principal advantage of the multi-programming feature is that a time-consuming job can be started and left running as a background job while the user goes on to do another job. For example, while a long text is being printed out on the printer, the next text can be input at the keyboard. The former is a background job and the latter is a foreground job. However, since there is a limit to the capacity of the computer, if too many users try to do too many jobs at once, the processing will be slowed down.

History of UNIX

Bell Laboratories, where UNIX was born, is a very large, world-famous laboratory, located in New Jersey. Since its establishment in 1925, it has been at the top level in the world in communications research.

In 1969, when UNIX was first developed, the Computing Science Research Division of Bell Laboratories was running an operating system called Multics on a General Electric 645 computer. Ken Thompson, who was a Multics user, wanted an operating system that would be easier

The DEC PDP-11/23
minicomputer

Computer language

UNIX is written in the C language

to use. He therefore developed a new one for himself. This operating system, called UNIX, was developed to make program development easier when several members of a project team are working on a single program, to make man-machine interaction easier and to be easier for beginners to use.

At that time Thompson was developing programs on a DEC PDP-7 minicomputer. He used the minicomputer because it was much cheaper to use than the large General Electric 645. However, since there was not much convenient software available for use on the PDP-7, he had to create his own. He set out to create a computing

UNIX system programs put out by AT&T

Name	Machines on which it can be used	Characteristics
MINI-UNIX	DEC PDP-11/10, 20, 34, 40	A scaled-down version of the standard UNIX; up to 13 tasks can be run at once
UNIX/V7	DEC PDP-11/45, 70	Can handle up to 40 users
UNIX/V6	DEC PDP-11/34, 40, 45, 70	Can handle up to 40 users
UNIX/32V	DEC VAX-11/780	The VAX version of V7; can handle up to 40 users
PWB/UNIX	DEC PDP-11/45, 70	An expanded version of UNIX/V6; has added features for use as a development system
UNIX SYSTEM III	DEC PDP-11/23, 34, 44, 45, 70 VAX-11/780	System III = V7 + PWB + some extras; can handle up to 48 users
UNIX SYSTEM V	PDP-11/70 VAX-11/780 VAX-11/750	Supported by AT&T; has greatly increased capabilities

environment that would suit his taste on the mini-computer. Thompson created an operating system, an assembler for use on the PDP-7, and a number of utility programs. However, since all of those programs were written in assembler code, they could not be easily transferred to another computer. This was inconvenient, so Thompson created the high-level language **B** and rewrote almost all the existing assembler programs in B.

Dennis Ritchie changed B extensively, to create an improved computer language called **C**. He rewrote the entire UNIX operating system in C. Characteristically, programs written in C are easily transferable from one computer to another. This feature is called portability. Since UNIX is written in C, it is also portable.

Once the operating system and C language were developed, the number of UNIX users gradually increased, and those users added their own improvements to the operating system and created new utility programs. This improved the capabilities of UNIX and gave it a more complete set of commands. Of course, these new programs were all written in the C language. The number of application programs for research and business use which run on UNIX also steadily increased.

Then AT&T, one of the owner companies of Bell Laboratories, began selling the system program license for UNIX.

Relation between different UNIX versions

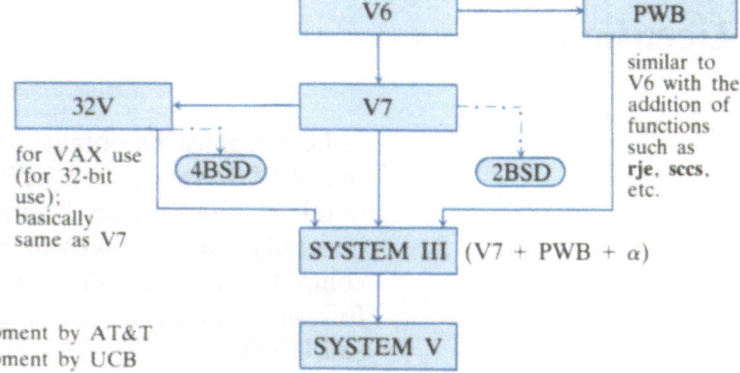

 UCB version
⟶ flow of version development by AT&T
– · – · – · → flow of version development by UCB

Even within the UNIX produced by AT&T, there are a number of different versions. It is apparent from the diagram that UNIX is steadily evolving.

In addition to the versions announced by AT&T, there are other versions put out by the University of California at Berkeley (UCB), which are further modifications of the AT&T versions, and which have become widely used. These versions include the letters BSD Berkeley Software Distribution) in their names.

The UCB version for use on the PDP-11, based on AT&T's V7, is called the 2BSD, and the UCB version for VAX use, resulting from considerable revision of AT&T's 32V, is called the 4BSD. These are available at cost to holders of the AT&T UNIX license. At present, the UCB versions 4BSD and 4.1BSD are widely used; the 4.2BSD was released late in 1983.

In the four UCB versions, a virtual storage capability has been added to the UNIX. Virtual storage management gives users a wider memory space than the actual (physical) one. The former is called a logical memory space. Virtual storage automatically accesses an auxiliary memory device such as a hard disc and swaps the contents of it with the contents of a main memory. The users need not know this swapping at all. They can just make programs as if they have wide memory area.

The command interpreter 'C Shell" and full-screen editor "vi" of the UCB versions are particularly popular.

Licensing

A license must be obtained from AT&T in order to use the AT&T version of UNIX. A company which has obtained a license for business purposes will eventually generally transfer UNIX to its own or another company's computer, and sell the combination. For example, the following companies are a few of those with licenses to sell UNIX.

Electronic Info System, Inc.
Interactive Systems, Inc.
Microsoft Corp.
UniSoft.
Wollongong Group, Inc.
Chuo Electronics Co., Ltd. (CEC)

The system is sometimes sold as it is under the name UNIX, but other names are sometimes used. For example, Microsoft calls its operating system called XENIX, and Interactive calls its system IS/1. Microsoft has transferred XENIX to the hardware of such companies as CM Technologies, Codata System, Micro Dasys, and so on. Interactive has expanded UNIX and added a number of office automation functions to form IS/1. CEC uses UNIX as the operating system for its own CEC8000 computer, and sells the computer and operating system together as a package.

UNIX became popularized largely through its use on DEC minicomputers. Now it appears that DEC itself will start to improve UNIX.

UNIX is sold under different names by different companies

Chapter 2
Computer Basics

This chapter explains the basic concepts of the computer
hardware, software, operating systems and other basics.

Basic Functions of Computer

Before a computer can function, information must be given to it. This information includes instructions to the computer on what to do, and the data to be processed. The operation of giving this information to the computer is called "**input**". This information is stored inside the computer. The location of this storage is called a **memory area**, and the device that contains the memory area is called a **memory device** or simply **memory**. The information is stored until the computer needs it. It is then sent to the **central processing unit** (abbreviated **CPU**), where it is operated on. In the CPU, instructions are decoded and data are processed in exact accordance with them. For example, the instructions might call for data to be brought to the CPU from a certain area in memory, and then multiplied by certain other specified data. This kind of processing is called an **operation**. The operations performed by the CPU are not limited to the four basic arithmetic operations, addition, subtraction, multiplication, and division. It also stores the data in memory, loads them to the CPU, compares two data and makes decisions based on the result, and so on.

The result of an operation is meaningless unless it is **output** somewhere. Sometimes it is output where it is immediately accessible to human eyes (such as a display screen and an electronic printer), but it can also be output

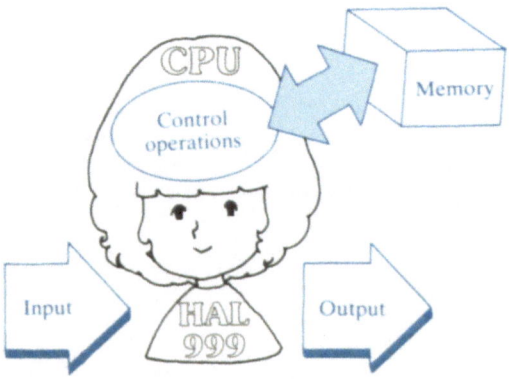

Basic functions of computer

to another memory device (such as a hard disc), where it is stored.

The last basic function is **control**. It controls, from the CPU, the other functions so that the computer can do meaningful work.

Thus, the computer has five basic functions:

> input
> memory
> operations
> output
> control

Components of Computer System

The many parts that make up a computer are combined into three principal types of units:

1. Central processing unit (CPU)
2. Memory devices $\begin{cases} \text{main memory unit} \\ \text{auxiliary memory units} \end{cases}$
3. Input/output (I/O) units

The CPU, which is analogous to the human brain, performs operations and control. The memory unit from which the CPU can read directly and into which the CPU can write directly is called the **main memory unit**. When very large or portable memory (e.g., magnetic tapes and floppy discs) is required, **auxiliary memory units** are connected to the computer. Since the main memory unit is inside the main body of the computer, it is called an internal memory. Auxiliary memory units, which are connected externally, are called **external** or **secondary memories**.

The amount of information that can be stored in a memory unit is called its **memory capacity**. Since memory units allowing the fastest access are highest in price, when memory is to be increased with little cost, units are added which cannot be accessed quickly. The main memory unit must have fast access, but if auxiliary memories are to be added then the main memory can have a relatively low capacity.

An **input/output device** (or I/O device) is literally for the input or output of information. It acts as the go-between between man and machine. There are a number of different types of I/O devices. In the following sections we will go into more detail on each of these groups of units and discuss what types are available.

An ordinary computer contains the CPU and main memory, and is surrounded by auxiliary memory units and input/output devices. These surroundings are called **peripheral devices**.

When peripheral devices are connected to a computer unit, it is necessary to make sure that information is transmitted between them. This adjustment is done by **interfaces**. Interfaces include a **channel** and a **multiplexer**.

Since input/output devices are very slow compared to the CPU, when the CPU is sending data to or receiving data from an input/output device, the CPU may become idle while waiting for I/O devices. Since this is a waste of CPU time, a small computer, used exclusively for handling input/output (called a **channel**), is sometimes used. With input/output left to the channel, the CPU is free to concentrate on other work, improving overall efficiency. **Multiplexers** selectively operate any of a number of input/output devices.

CPU

With the progress of technology, the elements which make up a CPU have progressed from vacuum tubes through transistors, ICs and LSIs (large-scale integrated circuits) to VLSIs (very large-scale integrated circuits).

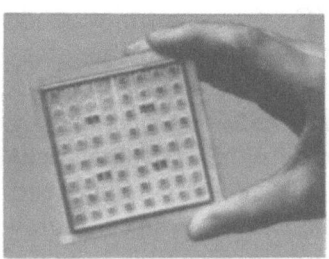

The high-density LSI package of the NEC ACOS System 1000

The type of CPU varies greatly, depending on whether it is to be used in a large computer, minicomputer or microcomputer.

The CPU of a microcomputer consists of one or more microprocessors. A microprocessor is sometimes called a CPU because it performs functions which include a CPU's functions. In computer designs using more than one microprocessor, there are advantages in terms of speed. Just as three people can sometimes think a problem through better than one thinking alone, several microprocessors working together can process data instructions faster than one. However, the complexity of the computer's design increases with the number of microprocessors used.

Most microprocessors perform 8- or 16-bit parallel processing. For a further discussion of bits, please refer to the section after next, on "Main Memory Units". The 8080, Z80 and 6809 CPUs are 8-bit, while the Z8000 and 68000 are 16-bit. The 16-bit CPUs process information faster than 8-bit CPUs, can directly access a greater memory area, and are able to handle complicated machine instructions with more functions than 8-bit CPUs. As instructions become more sophisticated, the hardware (in this case, the CPU) can do more sophisticated work, and the load on the software becomes lighter. Therefore it is convenient for creating an operating system or other software to use 16-bit CPUs.

The components of 8-bit CPUs are mainly LSIs, but 16-bit CPUs are still more highly integrated; they can probably be considered intermediate between LSIs and VLSIs. These LSIs are made of silicon semiconductor material using metal oxide semiconductor (MOS) technology.

Since large computers require very high speed, the LSI technology used in their CPU is different from that used for microcomputers. They use **bipolar technology**, which makes very high-speed processing possible. Large computers all have their own special CPU design, which makes matters more complicated than for a microcomputer. Many different types of LSIs are used (some are VLSIs but for convenience we will simply call them

LSIs). Commercially available ICs are sometimes used, but many are made in-house by the computer manufacturer.

In a microcomputer, ICs and LSIs are customarily mounted in a two-dimensional pattern on a printed circuit board, but in a large computer the need for high speed requires that the CPU and memory be more highly concentrated. The CPU is therefore assembled into a three-dimensional pattern, called a module, which contains many LSIs. This is necessary in order to shorten the distance travelled by the electrical signal, the limiting factor in computational speed. For example, the CPU module used in the Nippon Electric Corporation (NEC) ACOS System 1000 has LSIs mounted in a high density configuration as shown in the photograph below (NEC calls this a high-density LSI package). Each small square is a silicon chip LSI.

The definition of a minicomputer is somewhat vague. It lies somewhere between a microcomputer and a large computer. Minicomputers cover a very wide range, from small types having only slightly more capacity than a microcomputer up to what are called super types, which are really small versions of large computers. The CPUs of minicomputers are improved versions of the CPUs used in microcomputers.

Role of Memory

Because a CPU acts on information and instructions given it much faster than a human is capable of giving the information, the method, called the **stored program method**, of first storing a series of instructions in memory was developed. Then, once the execution of that series of instructions is started, as soon as each instruction is executed the CPU immediately calls the next instruction from memory, and executes it. Some CPUs execute one instruction and fetch the next at the same time.

At one time, every time the contents of the processing program were changed, the circuitry had to be altered, making it very troublesome to operate a computer. The stored program method makes it easy to make changes. The computer performs operations and control exactly in accordance with its instructions, so if something is wrong, the error almost invariably has to be in the program.

Main Memory Units

Main memory units contain the memory area that is directly accessed by the CPU, so media that can be accessed at high speed are used. There are almost always ICs and LSIs.

The smallest unit of information is called a **bit**, which has the value of either 0 or 1. When the CPU accesses memory, it is necessary to specify which location in memory is to be accessed, so it is necessary to have a method of identifying different locations in memory. The CPU classifies bits in memory into groups and then assigns a number (0, 1, 2, 3, . . .) to each such group.

Since the computer follows the directions in the program exactly, if it isn't doing what it is supposed to, the problem must be in the program

This number is similar to the address of a house on a street, so it is called an **address**. The CPU accesses one address in memory at a time; for example, it might retrieve the content of location 478211 in memory. CPUs are classified according to how many bits form one such group in memory (8 bits, 16 bits, 32 bits, etc.).

There are two types of memory ICs, called **RAM** (random access memory) and **ROM** (read only memory).

The existing contents of a RAM can be read out, and new contents can be written in. Programs and data are stored on a RAM. When a program is executed, the CPU rewrites the contents of the RAM as necessary. However, the contents of a RAM are lost when the power supply is cut off. Therefore, in order to store the contents of the RAM for later use, one must rewrite them into an external memory which will not lose its contents when the power is cut off, or into a memory which can be switched to a backup source of power if necessary.

A ROM is different from a RAM in that new data cannot be written into a ROM; all that can be done is to read the existing contents out. A ROM is used to store programs that will be run frequently.

Auxiliary Memory Units

Floppy diskettes

Floppy Discs

A **floppy disc** (sometimes called a diskette) is a storage medium consisting of a polyester disc coated with a magnetic substance. Information is magnetically recorded on it in tracks that form concentric circles. Each track is divided into a number of sectors.

A floppy disc is kept in a protective jacket. Disc and jacket are inserted into the floppy disc unit together. The floppy disc unit, called a **disc drive**, contains a read/write head. The head moves to write or to read information already on the diskette. Floppy discs come in two differ-

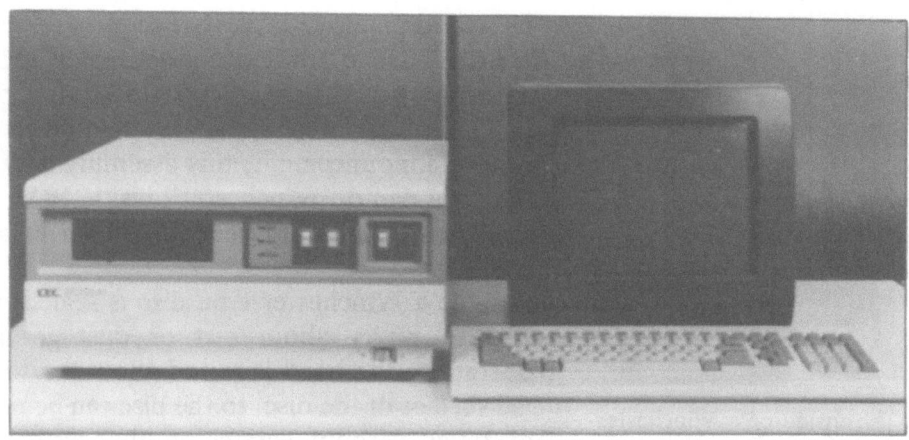

A desk-tope type 16-bit micro-computer. An 8-inch hard disc and a 5.25-inch floppy disc are built in the disc drive

ent sizes: 8 and 5.25 inches in diameter. An 8-inch disc is called a standard floppy disc, while a 5.25-inch disc is called a mini-floppy disc. Some diskettes are coated on both sides. These can be used to record twice as much information as diskettes which are only coated on one side. The memory capacity is on the order of 100 kilobytes to 1 megabyte (kilo = 10^3; mega = 10^6) (byte = 8 bits).

An 8-inch diskette, on which both surfaces are used, can hold about a million bytes of information. The floppy diskette drive is one type of popular auxiliary memory device.

Before a diskette can be used, it is necessary to write address information and other basic data onto it. This is called the **format**. Unfortunately the specifications of formats are not uniform; there are a number of different formats in use. However, most one-sided, single-density diskettes have already been initialized in IBM 3740 format, so they are ready to use.

Hard Discs
When one uses a full-fledged UNIX system, hard disc auxiliary memory becomes necessary. This offers faster access and larger memory capacity than the floppy disc. When the multi-user and multi-tasking capabilities of UNIX are used, the work load increases; a fast auxiliary memory unit becomes necessary. As the capabilities of UNIX increase, so does the number of programs;

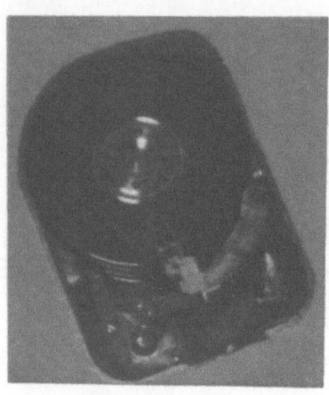

The inside of a Winchester-type hard disc drive looks like this

increased memory capacity becomes necessary.

In 1973, IBM announced the IBM 3340 hard disc drive, consisting of a disc, a read/write head, and an access arm (which moves the head), all enclosed in a sealed case. Before announcement, this assembly had been called by the code name "Winchester" inside IBM, so this type of sealed-case assembly became known as a "Winchester-type disc".

Since a Winchester-type disc is sealed, it is not necessary to worry about dirt or dust getting in. During operation, the head is raised about 0.5 to 0.7 micron off the surface of the disc, so the disc can be read any number of times without scratching the surface. This greatly improves the reliability. In the case of a regular floppy disc, the head is in contact with the disc surface during reading, so if the disc is read a large number of times it can become worn down.

The memory capacity of a Winchester-type disc is much larger than that of a floppy disc: several megabytes to several hundred megabytes. Also, the access speed is faster.

The first discs were 14 inches in diameter, but now discs having diameters of 8 inches and 5.25 inches have also been introduced. High-speed, large-capacity magnetic type memory devices exclusively for use in backup of discs have also recently come into use.

A floor-stand type CEC8000 SUPERBASE. The unit on the right contains a CPU, an 8-inch hard disc and a magnetic cartridge tape unit. The disc has a maximum memory capacity of 134 megabytes. The cartridge tape unit is used as backup for the hard disc

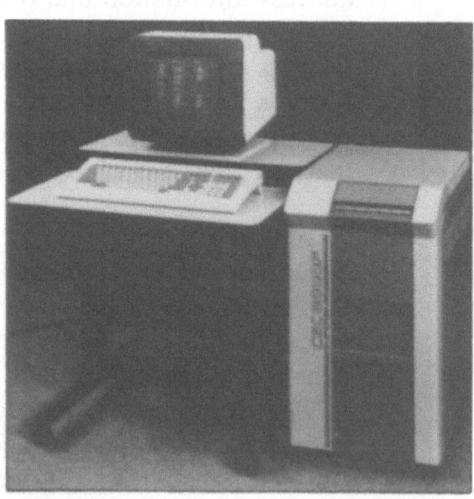

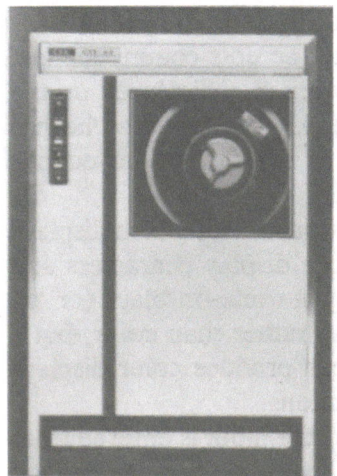

A magnetic tape unit. The tape can be seen in the window

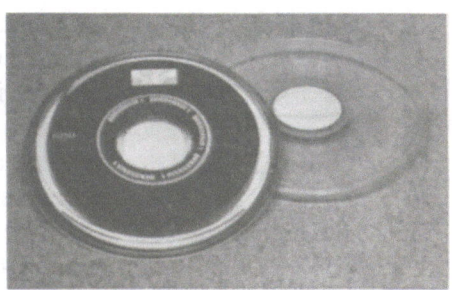

A magnetic tape

Magnetic Tape

The magnetic tapes used in computers can be thought of as an enlarged version of audio cartridge tapes. They are used frequently with large computers and minicomputers.

A magnetic tape consists of a magnetic coating on a plastic base. Information is magnetically recorded on the tape. Random access is slow compared to disc units, but since the cost of the medium per one bit of storage capacity is small and sequential transfer is fast, this type of unit is widely used for storing large quantities of data.

Input/Output Units

A standard terminal consisting of a CRT display and a keyboard

Since the user interacts with the computer through input/output devices, these are the units that are the most familiar to most users. We will discuss those units that are most likely to be used with a computer system on which UNIX runs.

Terminals

Since UNIX is an interactive operating system, all instructions which a user gives to the computer are input through a terminal. Each terminal has a keyboard through which the user communicates with the computer. Two types of terminals are frequently used: terminals with CRT displays, and terminals with teletypewriters.

A CRT display is similar to a television receiver.

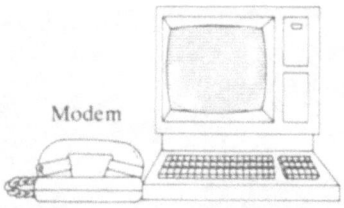

Modem

A modem is used to couple a computer to a telephone line

Output from the computer is displayed on the cathode ray tube (CRT). Once the computer accepts commands and other input from the user, they are also displayed on the CRT, so that the user can quickly see whether he has made a mistake. However, not all input that is keyed in is necessarily displayed on the CRT.

The CRT display is also an output device which displays output from the computer. It can display characters and pictures. The display is normally in white-on-black (or, on some machines, green-on-black) rather than color, but a CRT display for graphics use can produce color displays and have special graphics functions.

In the case of a teletypewriter, the input is entered from the typewriter keyboard, and the output is printed on paper set in the typewriter. This is somewhat uneconomical compared to a CRT because of the need to purchase the paper, but has the advantage that it leaves a record of what was done.

UNIX can be used with a number of different configurations of computer hardware. Some systems have a computer surrounded by several terminals. Others have only a terminal, and the user has to place a telephone call to link up with the computer.

A **modem** is necessary when using a telephone line to connect the computer and the terminal. A modem converts the digital signal from the computer or terminal into an analog signal for transmission over the telephone line, and, conversely, converts an analog signal from the telephone line into a digital signal for the computer or terminal.

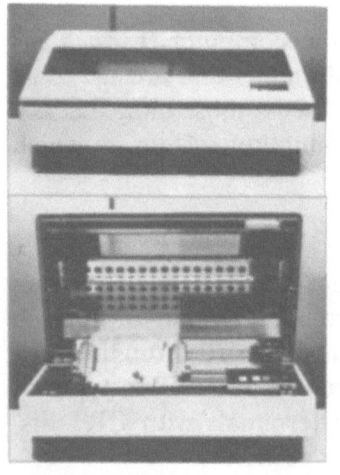

A printer with the cover raised

Printers
A **printer** is a device which prints characters out on paper. It is used for such purposes as to print the contents of a document file on a diskette, or to print out the listing of a program. In business operations, a printer might, for example, print budget reports and detailed payroll reports. There are printers of different quality, the principal differences being in the speed of printing and the appearance of the characters.

An X-Y plotter (photo courtesy
of Graphtec Corp.)

X-Y Plotters
An X-Y plotter is an output device which draws graphs
and geometrical figures. Characters can also be drawn;
the plotter draws each character like a geometrical figure,
rather than printing it all at once. A pen draws each figure
in two dimensions, driven by a controlled motor, just as a
person would draw it with a regular pen. A printer can
have several pens filled with different color inks, making it
possible to produce multicolored drawings. There are
some plotters that can change colors automatically.

Programs

Programs are necessary to make a computer function. A
program must be written in a special programming language that the computer can understand. The computer
stores the program in memory and then executes the steps
one at a time, calling each instruction from memory when
the previous instruction has been executed.

Programs are written by people. The computer executes a program exactly as it is written; if the person who
wrote the program made a mistake then the computer
executes the erroneous instruction as it stands. A mistake
of this kind in a program is called a **bug**. The process of
discovering bugs and removing them in order to produce a
correct program is called **debugging**.

Computer Languages

There are a number of different languages used for writing programs. For example, COBOL is often used for writing business programs. FORTRAN is often used for writing programs that perform numerical calculations, and LISP is often used in artificial intelligence. A language called PASCAL makes it possible to do structured programming. The C language was developed by the people who created UNIX. UNIX itself is written in C, so a necessary condition to be able to use UNIX is that C must run on the computer hardware being used.

There are numerous computer languages in existence. Most of us only know about the more famous ones. Each language has its own special characteristics. For example, the characteristics of C are that the contents of a program are easy to understand when the program is read out (structured programs can be written), and that bit operations, in which even the way the hardware is to operate can be specified, are possible.

All of the languages listed above are designed so that people can understand them easily. Such a language is called a **high-level language**. "High-level" means that a language is easy for a person to understand. A computer only understands its own special **machine language**, which is very hard for a person to understand. A machine language is called a **low-level language**. A program written in a machine language is just a bit stream, so for

If you start to speak in your native language to a foreigner who doesn't understand the language, you won't be understood. Similarly, if you try to talk to a computer that only understands a machine language in a high-level language, it won't understand you. So you need a translator, or translation program, that translates the high-level language into the machine language. There are two types of translators, compilers and interpreters

The flow of operations
in compilation

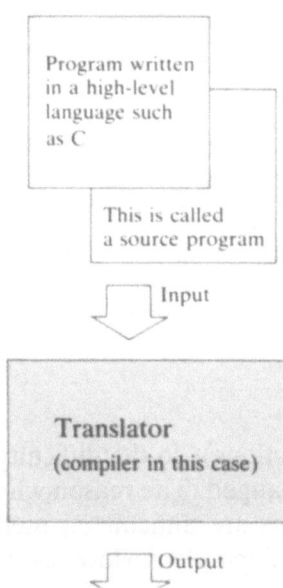

Input

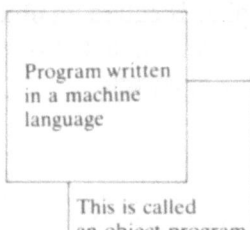

Output

a person to write a program directly in the machine language requires a great deal of effort. When computers were first developed, only machine languages existed; high-level languages that are easier for people to understand were developed only later. C is such a high-level language.

A computer cannot directly understand a high-level language. A program written in such a language must be **translated** to convert it into a program in machine language that the computer can understand. Who translates it? A program performs the translation. For example, a user writes a C program and input it into the C translator. The C translator converts the program in C into a program in machine language.

The creation of a new computer language involves not only the design of the language specifications, but also the creation of this translation program.

There are two ways of translating a high-level-language program into a machine-language program. One is to convert the whole program into machine language right away. This machine language program is stored in memory, and subsequent execution of the program is done by executing the machine language program. This is called the compilation method, and the translation program is called a **compiler**. The other method is to translate one instruction word, execute it and then go on to translate the next instruction word. This is called the interpretation method, and the program is called an **interpreter**. The translation programs are named according to the high-level languages which they translate: "C compiler", "FORTRAN compiler", "LISP interpreter", "BASIC interpreter", etc. Some languages have both a compiler and an interpreter.

A machine language consists entirely of a bit stream. To make a machine language program easier for people to understand, it is sometimes written in what is called an **assembly language**. Assembly language expresses machine language instructions in abbreviated English words instead of numbers, making the program easier for people to read. However, one instruction still corresponds to one instruction in machine language (and the

There are many computer languages, just like there are many stars in the sky, but it is only the best-known and most widely used languages that we are usually aware of

instructions perform the same functions), so the difficulty of programming is practically unchanged. The reason why writing machine language programs are difficult for men is that there are many machine dependent (low level) concepts in them.

The program produced by a compiler is called an **object program**. The original program written in a high-level computer language is called a **source program**.

How an Operating System Works

An operating system is a program that makes a bare machine (hardware) work like a real computer. An operating system consists of a **kernel**, which controls the basic operation of the computer, utility programs which run on it, and so on.

The kernel is always stored in main memory, and supervises all operations of the computer, including both hardware and software such as disc access scheduling, management of the file system, and task management. The user's commands which are entered from a terminal are read in, the necessary programs and data are called from auxiliary memory, and the programs are executed. If an input or output device is used while the system is running, the program requests the operating system to perform that input or output.

The control provided by the operating system can make a big difference in how efficiently the computer runs. The purpose of the operating system is to make sure that the **resources** of the computer system are used as efficiently as possible. If the control provided by the operating system is poor, the resources will not be used efficiently. "Resources" include everything needed to make the computer work. For example, the components of the hardware are resources. If the computer is used in such a way that CPU time is not wasted, then that particular resource has been used efficiently. The same is true of peripheral devices. The various programs, data and so on are software resources. We also speak of human resources, meaning the programmers, computer operators and supervisors. The effective use of human resources requires that people not be tied up doing routine operations. These should be done by the computer as much as possible. Also, making the computer easy to use helps

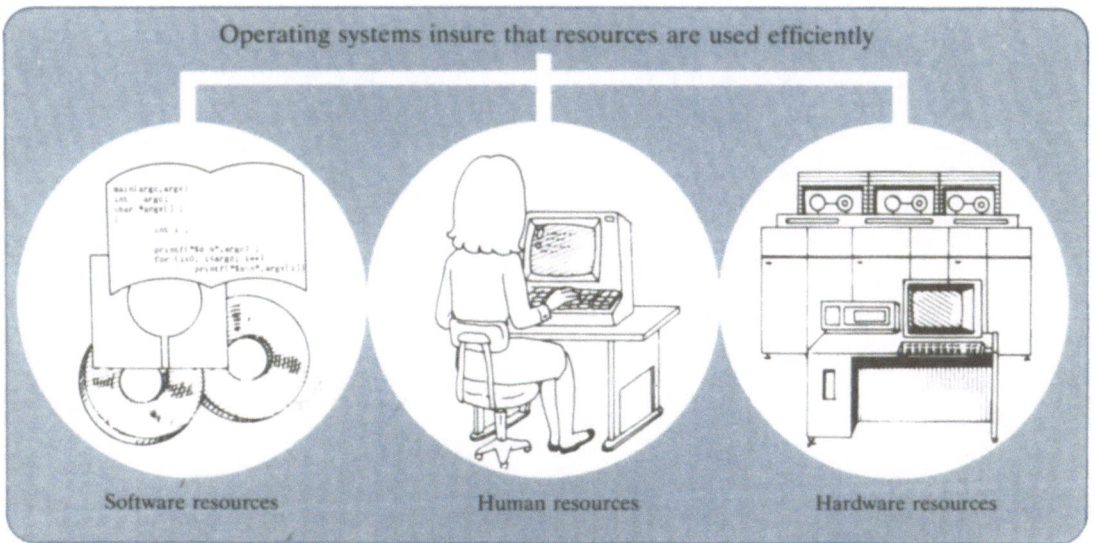

Operating systems insure that resources are used efficiently

Software resources   Human resources   Hardware resources keep people from getting tired. All resources are valuable and should be used as efficiently as possible.

Since the principal function of an operating system is supervision, in a narrow sense the kernel by itself could be considered the operating system (the kernel is, in fact, sometimes called the operating system in the narrow sense). However, it has become customary to consider the operating system to include a number of utility programs (the operating system in the broad sense, or simply the operating system). The utilities are basic programs which the user needs, such as the programs in the computer language processing system (editor, translator, etc.). There are also what are called "application programs", which perform a more restricted range of functions than the utilities. The usual programs prepared by a user are application programs. The boundary between utility programs and application programs is not always clear. It is sometimes hard to determine exactly whether a program is fundamental to the system or is only for a restricted purpose.

It is not an exaggeration to say that the creation of a favorable environment for program development and operation depends more on the operating system than on the hardware.

Chapter 3
Examples of the Use of UNIX

In this chapter we will see a number of examples of how UNIX is used. The topics we will discuss are grouped into the categories of office automation, program development and machine control. First let us look at some specific examples which illustrate the advantages offered by UNIX.

OFFICE AUTOMATION

Office Automation Using UNIX

We are seeing a dramatic increase in office automation, the introduction of computers into offices to save labor and provide services that were not possible previously. The functions that must be performed by office automation systems include the preparation of documents, electronic mail, business calculations, use of a data base, shared file systems, supervision of business operations, etc. The machines used in office automation are centered on computers—office computers, minicomputers and personal computers—and include word processors, microfilm units, optical disc image processors, laser printers, graphic terminals, audio input and output devices and facsimile machines.

To get the most out of all these devices, they must be combined into unified systems. For example, a word

An office automated with UNIX

With a UNIX machine
I can create documents,
send electronic mail,
do business calculations,
supervise files, supervise
office operations,
etc., etc.

I guess
I'll put one
in my office

processor is not used alone; rather, files stored in a computer are corrected by the word processor and the results are again stored in the computer, perhaps to be distributed to all employees in a division of a company by electronic mail.

Office automation systems using UNIX are steadily increasing in popularity. UNIX systems provide the office with such convenient capabilities as file sharing, document creation, information search using a data base, electronic mail, business calculations and so on. UNIX makes it possible to combine these into a unified system, providing combined capabilities not possible with devices used separately.

Let us consider some of these capabilities and see what role UNIX plays.

Work Stations

In a fully automated office, an employee's "work station" is a computer terminal. Most operations which were previously done sitting at a desk can now be done sitting at a computer terminal. A terminal includes a CRT display and a keyboard. The employee gives the UNIX system instructions from this terminal.

The employee first turns the terminal on and confirms that it is connected to the main computer on which UNIX runs; then he enters his own "log-in name". UNIX checks the name to make sure that the employee is a properly registered user, since only registered users are allowed to use the system. In many systems, the user must also enter his secret password to prove his identity.

The employee can now perform many different types of work while watching the CRT display. Documents, for example, can be prepared on the display before being printed out. Electronic mail from other people can be read on the display. Tables and graphs can be prepared on the display and checked to make sure that they are correct before being printed out, greatly cutting down on the use of paper. This kind of relatively "paperless" office makes it possible to economize greatly on the cost of paper and on space required for file cabinets. Of course, the computer on which UNIX runs is connected to a printer in case output on paper is desired, and any number of copies can be printed.

Sharing of Files

As our society becomes more complex, the amount of information that must be handled by individuals and companies has been growing by leaps and bounds. As the amount of information increases, the problem of access to the information you want when you want it increases also. If information supervision is poor, a great deal of time can be wasted looking for information and sometimes great trouble is caused because it cannot be found at all.

When UNIX is used to file information, all files[1] are stored in a hierarchical tree structure file system.[2] This makes the relationship between files easy to understand, and it becomes possible to find the file that you want easily. When searching for a certain file, the use of search keys, such as file name, creator, date of creation, size, etc. in combination greatly helps in finding it.

In principle, UNIX files are shared by all the users of the system. It is possible for someone other than the person who created a file to use it. All of the files in existence then become a shared resource which grows as more files are created. Within a company, for example, it might be necessary to prepare a great many different documents in a similar format. With this system, an employee can search for an existing document in that format and merely alter it to meet his needs, rather than having to create a new one from scratch. All file processing can be done while sitting at the terminal, making it unnecessary to walk around the office looking through file

1 File: information or a location where that information is stored in an auxiliary memory device
2 Hierarchical tree structure file system: refer to the discussion of this topic in Chapter 4

cabinets. The user is liberated from a mountain of documents, and from the need to carry them from one place to another.

Sometimes, of course, there are documents that you do not want to share with other people, and it becomes necessary for the system to have a **protection capability**. UNIX has a practically sufficient protection capability. For each file, reading the file, writing in it and executing it can each be separately permitted or not permitted for three separate categories of user: the owner of the file, user group, and others. A supervisor who administers a UNIX system can read all files in it, but the owner of the file can encode its contents using his own keyword. Then even the supervisor cannot understand it, though he can look at it.

UNIX, and in fact almost all computer systems, store files in peripheral memory units. One disc can hold information that would require hundreds of pages of paper. The amount of physical space required for filing is thus greatly decreased.

UNIX is designed to make it easy to reduce the amount of memory capacity required. For example, if one file is altered slightly to create a new file, it is not necessary to store the entire new file; only the information that was altered need be stored. The file which contains only parts of another file that have been altered is called a **differential file**. This greatly reduces the amount of memory occupied by files. To obtain the whole file, the differential file can be combined with the original file to produce the correct full file. Since most documents produced in offices are alterations of previous documents, this capability greatly reduces the amount of filing space required.

Since file operations can all be done sitting at a terminal, the sight of a secretary walking around an office with a load of paper files will gradually disappear

Electronic Mail

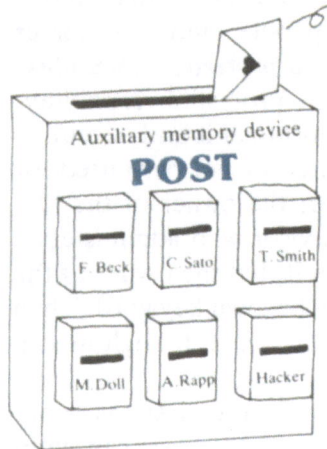

Each user has his own mailbox file on an auxiliary memory device

UNIX has an **electronic mail** function, and between users documents, messages and reports can be sent and received. These are files which are created by the editor and other programs. Files can be stored in an auxiliary memory unit, and each user has his own mailbox file on an auxiliary memory unit. When electronic mail is sent to someone, it accumulates in his mailbox file. It is possible to send electronic mail to two or more users simultaneously. The file which is sent can be one which has been created in advance by using the editor program, or it can be input directly from the keyboard at the time it is sent.

If a user receives mail, the next time he logs in to the system the message "you have mail" will appear on the CRT display. The user can decide whether or not to read it right away. The "letter" remains in the mailbox file until the user handles it.

When the user decides to have mail appear on the CRT display so he can read it, first the sender's name and the date it was sent are displayed; the contents follow. At the end of the letter the computer asks the user whether to store it or erase it. In the case of storage, the user has the choice of whether to leave it in the mailbox file or store it in his own separate storage file. It can also be output to a printer to be printed out on paper. The mailbox is protected so that other people cannot read what is in it.[1]

In contrast to the telephone, electronic mail never has the problem that the telephone is busy, so a letter can be sent at any time. The receiver does not have to interrupt his work to receive mail as he does with a telephone call; he can see his mail whenever he wants to.

Electronic mail has the advantage over regular mail that the work of delivering it to the receiver's address is eliminated. Also, it simplifies the problem of communication between people who work in different time zones. Progress in work and changes of plans can be communicated easily without face to face contact.

The ability to send files freely greatly increases the

1 As is discussed in Chapter 4, in the section on "Control of User Access", when someone else uses UNIX under your login name, mail can be read out freely

Electronic mail

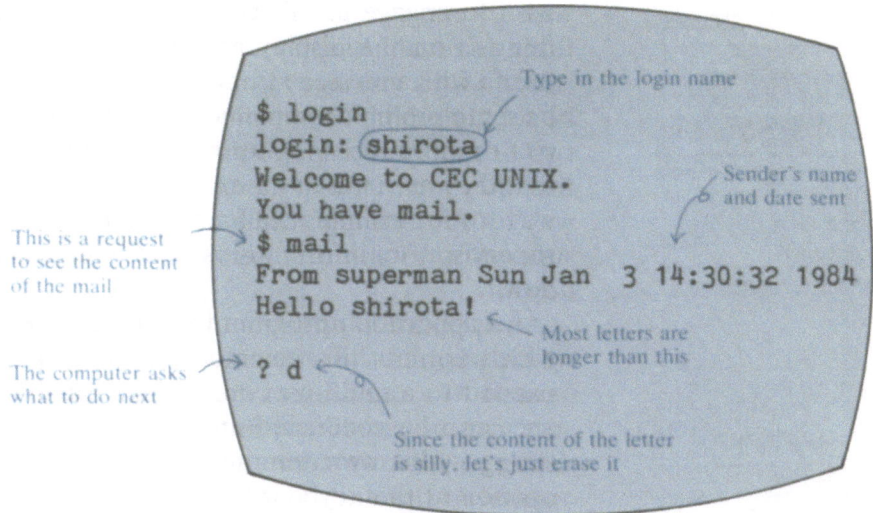

Type in the login name

```
$ login
login: (shirota)
Welcome to CEC UNIX.
You have mail.
$ mail
From superman Sun Jan  3 14:30:32 1984
Hello shirota!
? d
```

This is a request to see the content of the mail

Sender's name and date sent

Most letters are longer than this

The computer asks what to do next

Since the content of the letter is silly, let's just erase it

efficiency of office work. For example, a document which is needed for a meeting, which formerly had to be copied and then distributed to a number of people one at a time, can now be sent to everyone simultaneously by electronic mail. Only those people who really need copies will print them, saving greatly on the amount of paper used. Circulation of documents within a company and obtaining a superior's approval are just two examples of what can be done by electronic mail.

Communication between Terminals

UNIX permits users who are using a computer at the same time to communicate with each other via their CRT displays and keyboards. One user sends a message which appears on the display of the other, and then the second user can send a return message which appears on the display of the first. It does take time to send a message this way, but a fast typist is not likely to feel inconvenienced. If a user is busy with his work and does not

UNIX permits users who are
sitting at their respective terminals to exchange messages

wish to engage in this type of conversation, or if something is on the display and it is undesirable to have it
mixed with a message from another user, the terminal can
be set to prohibit communication. Messages can be sent to
two or more receiving terminals simultaneously provided
that they are in use at the time, making this a convenient
way to, for example, call a conference, or for the system
supervisor to inform users that the computer will be
down.

An application program for UNIX systems is available
which permits this communication capability to be expanded to a multi-user conference capability. A conference can be conducted among a number of users each
sitting at his own terminal. Each person can input his
opinion at the keyboard, and it immediately appears on
all of the display screens, including his own. At the end of
the conference, each user can then store his own copy of
the proceedings in a storage file.

Use of "write" for communication between terminals

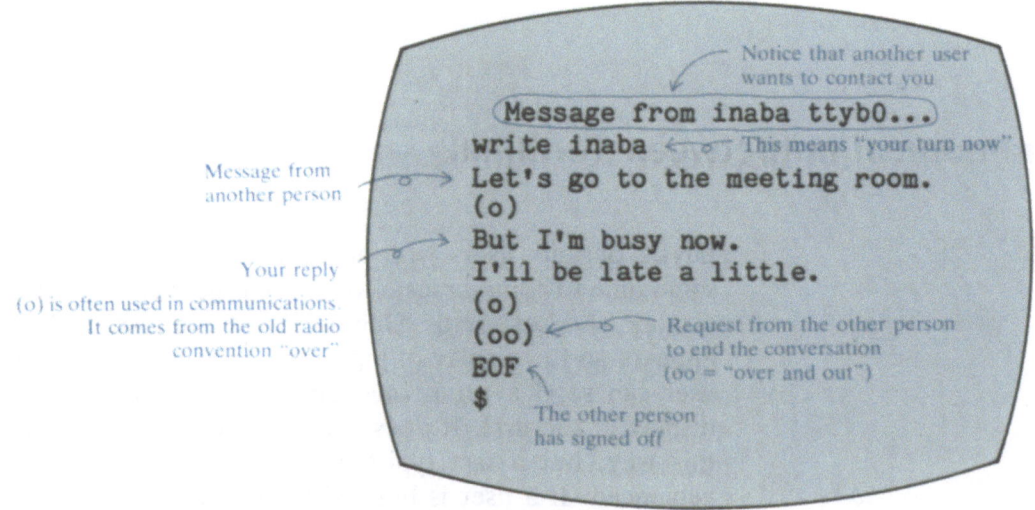

Word Processors

Considering the fact that with a conventional typewriter it is often necessary to retype a whole page on account of a mistake of a single letter, to waste a lot of time painting white correction liquid on the paper and waiting for it to dry, or to erase one letter at a time with a correction key, we can see what a convenient machine a **word processor** is. The word processor is becoming one of the three status symbols of a truly modern office, along with the computer and the facsimile machine. Thanks to the word processor, the time required to produce a document has been greatly reduced, and it is easy to produce a finished document unblemished in appearance.

Originally, the term "word processor" referred to a machine that was used exclusively for producing documents, but recently more and more computers are coming to have a word processing capability as merely one of their applications. The UNIX system has a **document preparation and touching up function** (formatting). Normally the editor is used to produce a file, and then an application program designed specifically for touching up documents is used to produce a clean, neat document. The editor is used not only to produce documents, but also for other purposes such as input of programs, so its discussion will be deferred until a later section where the system utilities are discussed, and here we will concentrate on explaining the application program used for touching up.

The following are some typical UNIX word processor programs:

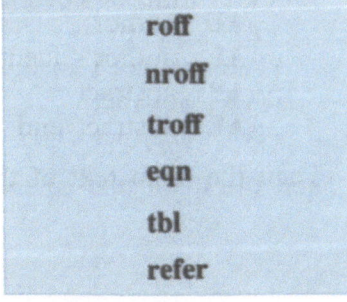

roff

nroff

troff

eqn

tbl

refer

roff, **nroff**, and **troff** are all programs used for touching up documents. **roff** produces output files for use with an ordinary line printer, **nroff** produces output files which can use the extra features of a somewhat better qualify printer, and **troff** produces output files for use with phototypesetters. The output produced by **troff** can be either sent directly to a phototypesetter or first output to an intermediate medium such as a disc, and the touched-up printing plate is produced in a short time from the disc file. **eqn** is for use exclusively with mathematical formulas and equations, **tbl** is designed for the preparation of neat tables, and **refer** is a program used for preparing bibliographies.

nroff and **troff** are nearly identical, and it is possible to use a printer for test printing of pages before they are set in type. It takes time to learn to use the many primitive functions of **nroff** and **troff** well enough to be able to produce documents in any format you desire, so standard specifications packages (**ms**, **mm**, etc.) are provided. These are generally sufficient except for very specialized documents.

Commands are inserted into the text of the documents to specify the touch-up format. Commands can be inserted by the editor, but it is possible to input sentences and commands together at the beginning if desired. Commands start with dots to distinguish them from sentences, and it is possible to remove the commands, leaving only the sentences.

For example, when a standard specifications package "**ms**" is used, the first part of a document looks like the following:

· **TL**   title of document
· **AU**   author
· **AI**   author's institution
· **AB**   abstract
· **AE**   abstract end

Then the main text of the document follows.

Sample document created with a standard specification macro package[1]

```
                    IV. Definition of PICCOLO

Extension of the relational model to satisfy Requirement 3.
     As explained in the previous section, the capability to represent an  ob-
ject,  a  relationship  and a relationship among relationships is required for
the framework.  To represent them, the relational model  proposed  by  Codd[6]
was extended and named PICCOLO.


Definition of PICCOLO
     A relation R in PICCOLO is defined as follows:
     R$$NxN[1]xR[1]xN[2]xR[2]x...xN[k]xR[k]xD[1]xD[2]x...xD[m]
     where N, N[i] are tuple id domains,
           R[i] is a set of relation names, and
           D[i] is a domain.

Suppose  that   t=(n,n[1],r[1],n[2],r[2],...,n[k],r[k],d[1],d[2],...,d[m])$$R.
Then,  n  is a tuple id given to the tuple t, n[i] and r[i] are used as a pair
to specify another tuple of a relation r[i] with a tuple id n[i],  d[i]  is  a
value  associated to the tuple t.  The tuple t represents a k-ary relationship
among  tuples  which  are  specified  by  (n[1],r[1]),  (n[2],r[2]),  ...,  and
(n[k],r[k]).  From the uniqueness of the tuple id in a same relation, the next
condition has to hold.
     $$t,t'$$R((n,...)=t$$(n',...)=t'$$n=n'$$t=t').
     But we do not impose stronger condition that asserts  the  uniqueness  of
the tuple id in different relations.
     $$t$$R$$t'$$R'((n,...)=t$$(n',...)=t'$$n=n'$$t=t'$$R=R').
     That is, a tuple id is not unique in the database except within one rela-
tion.   Hence, it is necessary to use a pair (n[i],r[i]) to specify a tuple in
the database.  By defining tuple ids relative to each relation, the modularity
of the system increases.
     The values of a tuple id domain are system defined except in  case  of  a
generic  tuple,  and  hence  invisible  to the users.  Other domains are called
visible.  In this definition, N, N[i] are invisible domains, and R[i] and D[i]
are  visible  domains.   To visualize what is represented by a tuple, we illus-
trate    it    as    Figure    3.     In    this    figure,    a    tuple
(n,n[1],r[1],n[2],r[2],n[3],r[3],  d[1],d[2],...,d[m]) is illustrated.  A pair
(n[i],r[i]) is represented by an arrow to the specified tuple.  A value is not
described explicitly if the value is not concerned.

Restriction to PICCOLO
     PICCOLO is quite general and it is possible to write an  abnormal  tuples
such  as  shown in Figure 4.  To inhibit the abnormal cases, for error preven-
tion, and to ease integrity assurance tasks, we defined a subclass of  PICCOLO
which  does  not  allow  the  abnormal  cases  and  is still general enough to
represent relationships among relationships.  The subclass of PICCOLO  defined
here is an n-stratified PICCOLO which is explained below.
```

1 Excerpted from "Logic for a Picture Database Computer and Its
  Implementation" by K. Yamaguchi and T.L. Kunii, Department of
  Information Science, Faculty of Science, The University of Tokyo

nroff has capabilities such as:

· Right alignment, center alignment, left alignment
· Specification of type
    boldface
    italics
· Specification of underlining
· Specification of pitch
· Addition of footnotes
· Drawing of boxes
· Specification of format
    margins
    column width
    width of blanks

   ms has the following capabilities to use in producing clean, neat documents.

· Titles
    headings
    subtitles
    specification of the position where the title appears (right, center, left)
    automatic page numbering
· Multiple columns
· Paragraph headings
    automatic boldface or gothic script
    automatic indentation
    automatic counting of paragraph numbers

   nroff and **troff** have many other capabilities in addition to those provided by **ms**.

   eqn is a program for phototypesetting of complicated mathematical formulas and equations, and **neqn** is a similar program for use with printer output. These programs are very useful in departments of science and engineering, where numerous papers containing mathematical formulas are written. These programs have capabilities such as those shown on the following pages. Readers who are not interested in the phototypesetting of mathematical formulas may skip the following explanation of **eqn**.

Principal Capabilities of EQN

· Greek letters (capitals and lower case)

$$\text{pi} \rightarrow \pi$$

· Special symbols
(The character strings on the left are converted to the symbols on the right through **eqn.**)

inf	$\rightarrow \infty$	approx	$\rightarrow \approx$
half	$\rightarrow \frac{1}{2}$	$\ldots$	$\rightarrow \ldots$
grad	$\rightarrow \nabla$	!=	$\rightarrow \neq$
sum	$\rightarrow \Sigma$	+=	$\rightarrow \pm$
int	$\rightarrow \int$	==	$\rightarrow \equiv$
union	$\rightarrow \cup$	>=	$\rightarrow \geq$
inter	$\rightarrow \cap$	->	$\rightarrow \rightarrow$

· Specification of blanks

· Superscripts (powers) and subscripts

$$x \text{ sup } 2 \rightarrow x^2 \qquad x \text{ sub } i \rightarrow x_i$$

· Fractions

$$a + b + c \text{ over } \{a + b\} \rightarrow \frac{a + b + c}{a + b}$$

· Root symbols

$$\text{sqrt } xy \rightarrow \sqrt{xy}$$

· Summations, products, limits

· Specification of type

· Symbols to distinguish different variables expressed by the same letter

$$x \text{ tilde } \rightarrow \tilde{x} \qquad x \text{ hat } \rightarrow \hat{x}$$

· Braces

$$\text{left } \{a \text{ over } b \text{ right}\} \rightarrow \left\{ \frac{a}{b} \right\}$$

· Matrices

These format specifications and symbols are standard, in common use in writing research papers, making **eqn** very powerful and easy to use.

EQN output examples

Of course the best-looking printing is obtained by using **eqn** and **tbl** with a proper phototypesetter, but as long as the printer is a good enough model to have a half-spacing capability, output such as that shown here can be produced

Example 1

Program 1

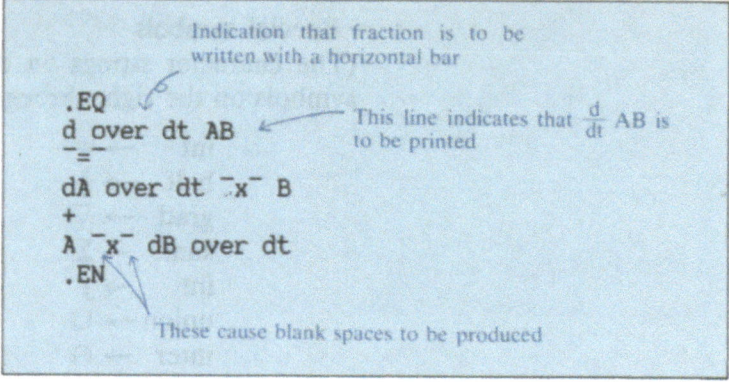

Output 1

$$\frac{d}{dt}AB \quad = \quad \frac{dA}{dt} \quad x \quad B + A \quad x \quad \frac{dB}{dt}$$

Example 2

Program 2

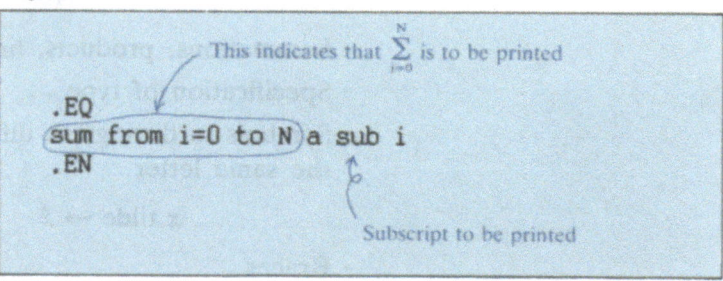

Output 2

$$\sum_{i=0}^{N} a_i$$

Example 3

Program 3

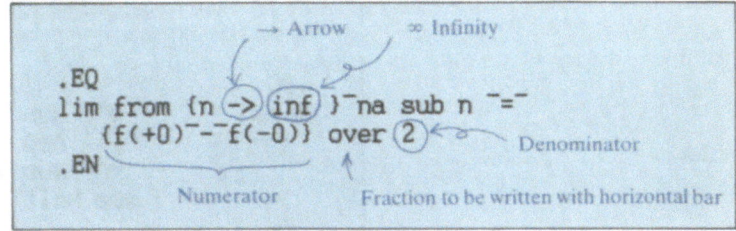

```
                        → Arrow        ∞ Infinity
.EQ
lim from {n -> inf }⁻na sub n ⁻=⁻
   {f(+0)⁻-⁻f(-0)} over 2
.EN
                                              Denominator
          Numerator       Fraction to be written with horizontal bar
```

Output 3

$$\lim_{n \to \infty} na_n = \frac{f(+0) - f(-0)}{2}$$

Example 4

Program 4

```
Left and right brackets
.EQ                    Superscript
{L sup -1}
left [                                    Denominator
pile {e sup {{-t sub 0} s} over s+a }
right ]
⁻=⁻
left{              Left brace                        First column
  lpile {0 above e sup {-a(t- t sub 0 )} }
⁻⁻lpile
   { if⁻t<{t sub 0} above if⁻{t sub 0}<t  }
.EN
                   Distinguishing between elements   Second column
```

Papers can be turned out easily too!

Output 4

$$L^{-1}\left[\frac{e^{-t_0 s}}{s+a}\right] = \begin{cases} 0 & \text{if} \quad t < t_0 \\ e^{-a(t-t_0)} & \text{if} \quad t_0 < t \end{cases}$$

Example 5

Program 5

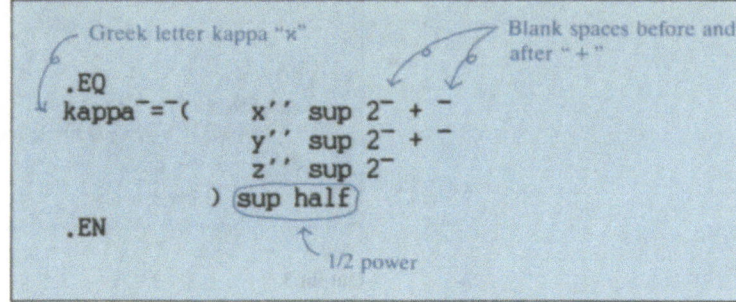

```
.EQ
kappa¯=¯(        x'' sup 2¯ + ¯
                 y'' sup 2¯ + ¯
                 z'' sup 2¯
           ) sup half
.EN
```

Greek letter kappa "κ"

Blank spaces before and after " + "

1/2 power

Output 5

$$\kappa \quad = \quad (\; x''2 \quad + \quad y''2 \quad + \quad z''2 \quad)1/2$$

Example 6

Program 6

```
.EQ
tau¯=¯1 over kappa sup 2
left |
    pile {x' above x'' above x'''}   ← First column
    pile {y' above y'' above y'''}   ← Second column
    pile {z' above z'' above z'''}   ← Third column
right |
.EN
```

Greek letter tau "τ"

Column notation

Vertical bars enclosing determinant

Output 6

$$\tau \quad = \quad \frac{1}{\kappa^2} \begin{vmatrix} x' & y' & z' \\ x'' & y'' & z'' \\ x''' & y''' & z''' \end{vmatrix}$$

tbl is a program which makes it easy to produce complicated tables. It has the following capabilities:

Box enclosures
Right alignment, center alignment, left alignment
Alignment of decimal points
Specification of type
Specification of table format

refer is a program used to produce bibliographies. In order to use **refer**, a data base of reference literature must be prepared in advance.

Here is an example of the English word list which UNIX contains. These are the word starting with "ab", as output by using UNIX's **look** command

ABA	abet	abound	absinthe
Ababa	abetted	about	absolute
aback	abetting	above	absolution
abalone	abeyance	aboveboard	absolve
abandon	abeyant	aboveground	absorb
abase	abhorred	abovementioned	absorbent
abash	abhorrent	abrade	absorption
abate	abide	Abraham	absorptive
abbas	Abidjan	Abram	abstain
abbe	Abigail	Abramson	abstention
abbey	abject	abrasion	abstinent
abbot	ablate	abrasive	abstract
Abbott	ablaze	abreact	abstractor
abbreviate	able	abreast	abstruse
abc	ablution	abridge	absurd
abdicate	Abner	abridgment	abuilding
abdomen	abnormal	abroad	abundant
abdominal	Abo	abrogate	abusable
abduct	aboard	abrupt	abuse
Abe	abode	abscess	abusive
abed	abolish	abscissa	abut
Abel	abolition	abscissae	abutted
Abelian	abominable	absence	abutting
Abelson	abominate	absent	abysmal
Aberdeen	aboriginal	absentee	abyss
Abernathy	aborigine	absenteeism	Abyssinia
aberrant	aborning	absentia	
aberrate	abort	absentminded	

Examples of tables produced by TBL

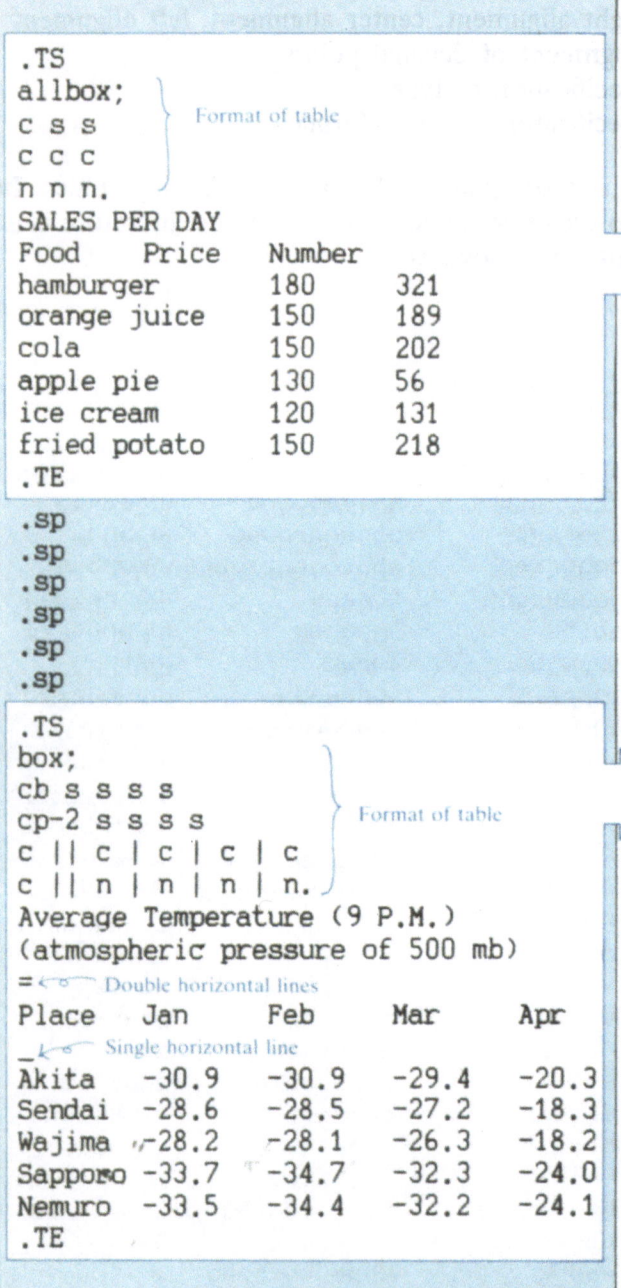

```
.TS
allbox;
c s s        } Format of table
c c c
n n n.
SALES PER DAY
Food      Price    Number
hamburger        180    321
orange juice     150    189
cola             150    202
apple pie        130    56
ice cream        120    131
fried potato     150    218
.TE

.sp
.sp
.sp
.sp
.sp
.sp

.TS
box;
cb s s s s
cp-2 s s s s     } Format of table
c || c | c | c | c
c || n | n | n | n.
Average Temperature (9 P.M.)
(atmospheric pressure of 500 mb)
= ←   Double horizontal lines
Place    Jan      Feb      Mar      Apr
_ ←   Single horizontal line
Akita    -30.9    -30.9    -29.4    -20.3
Sendai   -28.6    -28.5    -27.2    -18.3
Wajima   -28.2    -28.1    -26.3    -18.2
Sapporo  -33.7    -34.7    -32.3    -24.0
Nemuro   -33.5    -34.4    -32.2    -24.1
.TE
```

Result of output to printer

SALES PER DAY		
Food	Price	Number
hamburger	180	321
orange juice	150	189
cola	150	202
apple pie	130	56
ice cream	120	131
fried potato	150	218

These tables were produced using the program at the left

Result of output to printer

Average Temperature (9 P.M.) (atmospheric pressure of 500 mb)			
Place	Jan	Feb	Mar	Apr
Akita	-30.9	-30.9	-29.4	-20.3
Sendai	-28.6	-28.5	-27.2	-18.3
Wajima	-28.2	-28.1	-26.3	-18.2
Sapporo	-33.7	-34.7	-32.3	-24.0
Nemuro	-33.5	-34.4	-32.2	-24.1

-- CEC8000 SUPER COMPUTER --
SUMMARY

HARDWARE SPECIFICATION		
CPU = Z8001	Address space	8 Mbyte (max)
	Clock rate	4 MHz or 6 MHz
	Registers	16 x 16-bit
	Data types	bit, digit, byte, word, long word, byte string, word string
	Addressing modes	IM, R, IR, DA, X, RA, BA, BX
	Instruction sets	105
	Interrupts	3 levels, 128 vectors
Memory MMU = Z8010	Capacity	128/256/512 Kbyte
	Segments	128 x 64 Kbyte
	Protection	RD, EXC, CPUI, DMAI, SYS
Floppy disks	Capacity	4 x 1.2 Mbyte (max)
Winchester disks	Capacity	4 x 10/20/40 Mbyte (max)
Magnetic tape	Density	800/1600 BPI
Timers		3
Serial ports		10 RS232c's (max)
Parallel ports		1 (printer)
Terminals		10 (max)
	Screen	12 inch green phosphor CRT
	Display capacity	80 columns x 24 lines
	Transfer rate	9600 baud
	Character sets	95 ASCII printable, 31 graphic
	Keyboard	full ASCII, ten-key
Printer	Type	dot matrix impact printer
	Resolution	4,7 dots/mm
	Speed	180 characters/sec. (max)
	Dot mode	available

SOFTWARE SPECIFICATION		
Operating systems	UNIX	multi-user interactive OS
	UCSD Pascal	single-user interactive OS
Languages	UNIX	assembler, language C, FORTRAN, COBOL, BASIC
	UCSD Pascal	assembler, Pascal
Word processor	UNIX	editor, formatter, spelling corrector
	UCSD Pascal	editor
Office automation	UNIX	electronic mail, information retrieval
Graphics	UNIX	
DBMS	UNIX	SQL-like

Tables like this can be produced easily. This one looks like a summary of the computer specifications

UNIX permits these word processor programs to be combined to produce documents neat in appearance. UNIX offers the following advantages over a machine designed exclusively for use as a word processor.

- All files on UNIX can be used.
- Numerical calculations that appear in the text can be worked out.
- Output can be sent to any of a number of peripheral devices connected to the UNIX system.

UNIX is probably the best word processing system for preparing computer manuals, fancy business documents, papers in the sciences and engineering which include mathematical expressions, and other applications in a wide variety of fields.

UNIX contains an extensive English "dictionary" (words only, without meanings) which it uses to check for spelling mistakes. The computer checks to make sure whether all words in a document are in its dictionary; any that are not are displayed on the screen as possible cases of misspelling. It can also check the frequency with which words appear in the text and list those that are unlikely to appear as often as they do.

Data Base Management Systems

Data base management systems which run on UNIX include the famous **ingres** (INteractive Graphics and REtrieval System) developed at the University of California at Berkeley. **ingres** is a full-scale relational data base management system written in the C language using the **yacc** compiler-compiler.

The user uses a special language called **quel** (QUEry Language) to obtain the information which he needs from the data base, perform operations on it and convert it to a form that is suitable for his purposes. **quel** acts as an interface between users and a data base.

A relational data base stores information in the form of a table. Basic operations which can be performed on relational data bases include the combination of two or more data, retrieval of only those elements that meet certain conditions, and removing duplicate elements, leaving only those that are unique.

Suppose, for example, that we have a data base used for supervision of salaries and that it contains the following information about each employee:

- Name
- Department
- Monthly salary
- Date of birth
- Home town

Then, the following operations can be easily performed using the data base management system.

- All information concerning the employee named Richardson can be obtained.
- Names and monthly salaries of all people in the General Affairs Department and the Planning Department can be given.
- Monthly salaries of all people in the General Affairs Department aged 40 (as calculated from the date of birth) and over can be raised by a uniform £100.00-.
- A new data base containing the name of each employee and the amount of his or her bonus can be created. Six times the monthly salary (a typical annual bonus in Japanese companies) is used as the amount of the bonus.

Now let's see what the **quel** language of **ingres** is capable of. The conditional search capability can use such conditions as the following:

=	equal
! =	unequal
>, >=, <, <=	larger than, smaller than

These conditions can be combined logically to form the logical conditions "and", "or" and "not".

Items of information which satisfy the conditions can be arranged in any desired order. To create new items, in the case of numbers the following operations can be performed:

+	addition
×	subtraction
/	division
*	multiplication
**	raising to a power
abs	absolute value
mod	modulus (remainder of division)

The names of items can be changed, and new names can be created.

In the case of a conditional search, since there is a pattern matching function for character strings, mnemonic names can be used as keys.

Some other things that can be done include counting of the number of data that satisfy some condition, finding the maximum and minimum values of those data, averaging and summing. Statistical information can be obtained from tables very quickly using **avg** and **sum**. Items of information can be freely replaced, deleted and added. This kind of data base management system promises great improvement in the efficiency of office work.

There are also many other commercially available data base management systems which run on UNIX.

Computer Networks

As office automation progresses, it sometimes happens
that a single computer becomes insufficient, and it becomes necessary to connect two or more computers to
form a **computer network**. The mutual interactions of two
or more computers make it possible to use a larger
number of files, to increase the area over which electronic
mail can be sent, and to share both hardware and
software. Recently, networks have proven their usefulness in coordinating work by different members of a team.
A network can make it possible to access remote system's
devices. For example, a laser printer, an optical disc, a

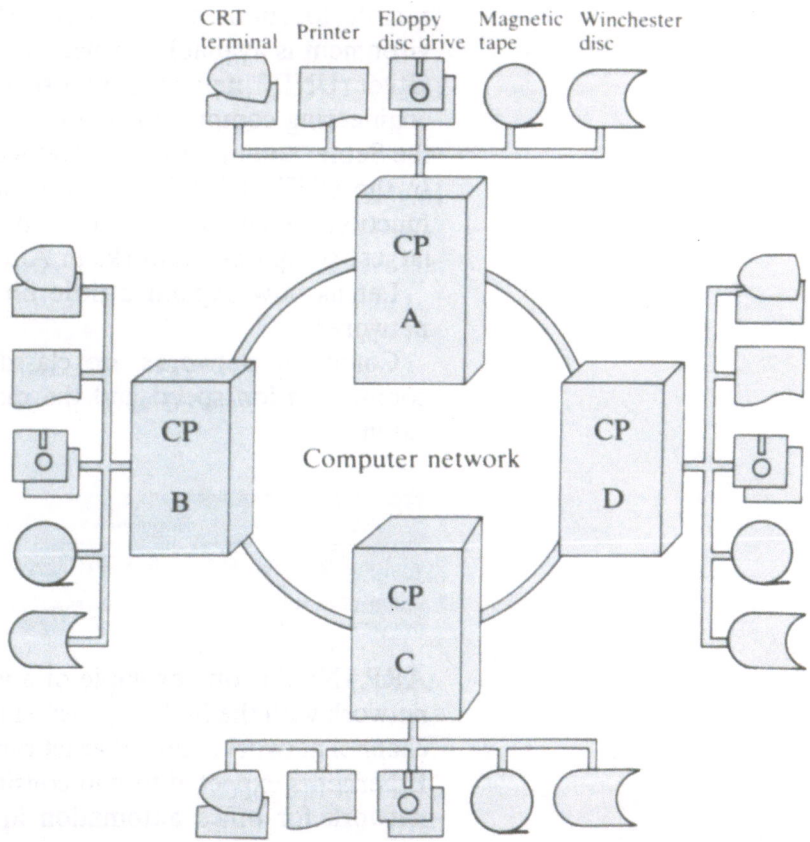

tape backup system, and a phototypesetter can be directly connected to certain remote computers.

UNIX has a communication capability that can be used for computers connected to each other either in-house or over a telephone line. For example, **uucp** transmits files between computers on which UNIX is running, and **uux** makes remote execution of commands possible. One UNIX system can call another UNIX, which in turn can call still another UNIX. In addition, there is **rje**, which can use an IBM/360 or 370 at a remote location from a computer which uses UNIX.

One UNIX computer network is the **Berknet** at the University of California at Berkeley. Several tens of large and small computers are connected to this network. Files are transmitted between these computers, remote execution of commands can be carried out, electronic mail is sent and received, and printers and phototypesetters at remote locations can be used. The same computer environment is available for use from anywhere on campus. Other UNIX networks in existence include the ECN engineering computer network at Purdue University and the Setnet computer network at Keio University in Japan. In the UNIX 4.2 BSD version, there are many network functions which are used in ARPANET, one of the largest computer networks in America.

Let us now explain a little bit more about computer networks.

Computer networks are classified according to their communication speed and the distance over which they extend.

	Speed	Distance
Wide-area network	10^3 to 10^5 bits/sec	Several km or more
Local area network	10^6 bits/sec or more	Several km or less

ARPANET is one example of a wide-area network. The network with the highest processing capacity is the Hyperchannel network, and **Ethernet** ranks about in the middle. Ethernet is expected to find considerable application as a network for office automation in the future.

Ethernet was first announced by Xerox Corporation in 1976, and in September, 1980, three companies, Xerox, Intel and DEC, announced common specifications. It is now the only local network for which the specifications have been made public. Over 100 companies, including such giants as IBM and AT&T, have purchased licenses to use Ethernet.

The 3Com Company, which is one of the makers of the OEM harware for Ethernet, has announced a program called UNET for use in carrying out communication on Ethernet. As you might guess from the name, it runs on UNIX. Another network, called LocalNet, put out by the Sytek Corporation, is a broad band local network that can send both computer and video signals over a wide range of frequencies. It is now used in many places, including the University of Utah. Local networks are becoming widely used in office automation, and many of these systems run on UNIX. For example, the University of Tokyo is running a computer/video conference system named Crossover Net using Local Net.

Several tens of companies have announced local networks, but not all have yet been put on the market and into actual operation. Some examples of local networks and the companies which make them are given in the table below.

Local network	Name of company
Ethernet	DEC, Intel, Xerox, 3 Com, AMD, Mostek, Zilog, and others
ARC	Datapoint
Hyperchannel	NSC
LocalNet	Sytek/NRC
Wangnet	Wang
Net/One	Ungermann Bass
Cluster/One	Nestar
Polynet	Logica
LCN	Control Data
Modway	Modcon Division of Gould
Omnilink	Northern Telecom
Primenet	Prime Computer
Z-Net	Zilog

Total Office Automation Systems

Running an office automation system on UNIX has the great advantage that software developed by the user can be incorporated into the system. Many word processors are sold for offices, but one's own business calculation programs will not run on them. This problem can be solved by using a general-purpose computer with UNIX, which can then be used for both word processing and business calculations.

It is inefficient to buy a variety of office automation machines which cannot be unified into a single system. In the future, it will become increasingly important to have integrated total systems for office automation.

Interactive Systems Corporation, one of the largest American makers of office automation equipment, has been promoting the use of UNIX for office automation. It uses a version of UNIX called IS/1 which includes an expanded word processor program called INword and an expanded editor called INed. This system can also handle communications both within a company and between companies.

Problems of Ideographic Word Processing

One of the biggest problems encountered by UNIX and other American operating systems is that while it can easily handle the Roman alphabet, it cannot handle the Japanese language or other languages which use the same characters, such as Korean and Chinese. This means that while UNIX is useful for word processing in Western countries such as the United States, it is not so useful in countries such as China, Korea and Japan. The word processing functions of UNIX include programs that check for errors in input from the keyboard, but these are useless with ideographs. The English word dictionary data base and the program that judges whether a word is "English-like" or not can only be used for English.

Computer users in Far Eastern countries are eagerly anticipating the day when an ideograph word processing capability will be added to UNIX. At present various experimental approaches are being tried.

Development of Office Automation Software ━━━━━━

A great deal of office automation software has been developed for use with UNIX, but it is only natural that sometimes it doesn't provide the satisfaction of software developed to exactly meet the needs of a particular company. Development of office work processing application programs is sometimes done in-house by the users themselves, but the work is often contracted out to software companies.

When specialized software is developed, the fact that UNIX is a superior software development system becomes very important. UNIX has a full lineup of software development tools and provides a programming environment in which it is easy to work, so that software can be developed with less difficulty than might otherwise be encountered. Another advantage of using UNIX is that software development can be done on the same hardware that is used for the office automation work itself. Since the same UNIX system is used for both, once the software is developed it can be immediately put to practical use.

PROGRAM DEVELOPMENT

Man-Machine Interfaces

UNIX provides a favorable environment for the user to develop new programs. One has the feeling that when one works on UNIX, the work will be easier and require less effort, and the program will be completed faster, than might otherwise be the case. This did not happen by accident. UNIX was developed by leading programmers at the Bell Telephone Laboratories who knew what kind of operating system would be easy to use and what kind of operating system they themselves, as the first users of it, would want. Some of the reasons why UNIX is easy to use are that input is easy, and a full lineup of software tools is provided.

Let us first look at what is meant by input being easy. The term **man-machine interface** has recently come into widespread use. The interface mediates between a man and a machine which are exchanging information. Since

Example of a shell procedure

```
for                                    for ~ do ~ done
        arg                            case ~ esac (opposite of "case")
do
        case $arg in
                /*)  echo 'cannot begin with /'; exit ;;
        esac
done
        umask 0
        /etc/mount /dev/fd1   /mnt1
        /bin/tar cf - $* | (cd /mnt1; /bin/tar xvf -)
        /etc/umount /dev/fd1
        /bin/sync
```

It's convenient to be able to do what you want to do just by combining commands

Even when the processing you want to do is complicated, it is not necessary to write a program from the beginning; often all that you need to do is combine existing commands

human languages and computer languages are different, the method which the man has to use to give instructions to the machine is unnatural and can be tiring. Therefore people have started to look for easier ways to communicate with machines, such as by voice communication. Perhaps voice communication would be easier than using a keyboard and CRT display. All of the hardware and software used to mediate between the man and machine, and translate from the man's language to the machine's language and vice versa, is called the man-machine interface.

In UNIX, commands are made very easy to use by a command interpreter named **shell**. At first commands are given to shell, and shell interprets them. After evaluating the command list, some commands are executed by calling the corresponding utility programs.

A user can create **shell procedures** which are the files containing commands. A shell procedure can be executed as an ordinary command by shell. A shell procedure can use variables and various types of control flow constructions just like high-level languages. UNIX commands can be called just like functions and subroutines, so that it is unnecessary to write special subprograms. All the user needs to do is combine commands to serve his needs. The use of shell procedures often saves considerable effort compared to using another high-level program to perform the same operation.

Easy-to-Use Files

The term "file" can refer either to a location into which programs, data and documents are entered, or to its contents. Ordinary files are stored magnetically on auxiliary storage devices.

In UNIX the entire file system forms what is called a **hierarchical tree structure**, making it easy for the user to supervise the files. Since the user can determine the structure of his own file area, he can decide on his own method of file supervision, such as grouping related files together.

One of the characteristic features of UNIX is that there is only one file format in which information can be stored. In UNIX a file consists of only a sequence of characters. In many other operating systems part of each file has to be taken up with markers to mark the beginning and end, and the information that is stored has to be divided up into records and blocks, so that a file cannot be used without specifying a number of parameters. And the format varies depending on the contents of the file, so that not all files can be handled the same way. It is troublesome to always have to worry about the formats of files. When using UNIX, on the other hand, it is not necessary to worry about the format of a file. This makes file access much easier. UNIX regards input and output devices as files, making them easy to use just by writing statements in the same manner as for files.

The reason for specifying formats with other operating systems is to increase the efficiency with which hardware is used. This also makes for more efficient operation of the disc heads which are used to access discs on which files are stored. In the case of UNIX, the simplified handling of files in programs results in a decrease of efficiency in the use of hardware, at least in the present versions of the system, and sometimes a head will wander all over a disc looking for data.

UNIX is an operating system which attaches greater importance to simplicity of programming than to the efficient use of hardware. When programming is done on UNIX, files can be handled easily and the writing of programs progresses rapidly, and some reduction in the efficiency of hardware use is simply accepted. Since hardware capable of ever higher speeds is becoming available at steadily dropping prices, when the drastic reduction in the amount of the programmer's nervous energy that is expended is taken into account, it is probably safe to say that UNIX is far more economical, on balance, than the other systems. And, of course, it is always possible to use UNIX as a development system to develop software that will use the hardware more

Since we introduced UNIX we have had fewer ulcers caused by writing programs!

efficiently than in the past, without loss of its ease of use for the programmer. For example, the recent SYSTEM V announced by AT&T has achieved a greater improvement in the efficient use of hardware.

Combining Programs

In dealing with UNIX we speak of a "flow" of data between programs, analogous to a flow of water. Data are input from one program and output to another. Just as a flow of water can be controlled by using pipes, the flow of data can be controlled by using programs that play a similar role to pipes. Just as a pipe has an entrance and exit for water, a program has a standard input port for data and a standard output port for data; the output port of one program can be connected to the input port of another.

Among the programs which perform the roles of pipes, there are some which the user writes himself and others which are provided as UNIX utilities. A typical program takes the flow of data from a standard input file, perform some operation on the data and then output them to a standard output file. The data are in the uniform UNIX file format, making it easy to write and combine programs.

Thus, UNIX has the feature that all processing done on UNIX is treated as a flow of data, but in fact there is a difference between the flow of data and the flow of water. When water flows somewhere it goes away and that's it, but in the case of data, even if the data are sent to an output device and hard copy is produced, the same data could still remain in a file.

PROGRAM

If you let water flow out it goes away and is lost, but data in a file can be copied and the same data still remain in the file

Programming Language C

When we think of UNIX as a software development system, we realize the important role played by the computer language C. UNIX itself was originally written in assembler language, but it was almost completely rewritten in the high-level computer programming language C in order to make it easier to transfer to other machines. Therefore, most programs that run on UNIX are written in C. This is not because other languages are particularly difficult to use, but it is most convenient to use C because of all of the software tools that are available for it.

C was created by one of the people who developed UNIX, expressly for the purpose of writing UNIX, and has a number of characteristic features.

Characteristic Features of C

> · Many types of data can be used.
> · Many types of operators can be used.
> · Many types of control flows can be used.
> · Seperate compiling can be done.
> · High-quality executable programs can be created.

Let us now explain these characteristic features of C one by one.

The many types of data which can be used by UNIX include characters, short integers, long integers, floating point, double-precision floating point, structures, arrays, functions, pointers, etc.

Then, there are many types of operators that can be used. Compared to other high-level languages, the ability of C to perform detailed bit processing is noteworthy. Since C is capable of highly detailed descriptions, some software which previously had to be written in assembler language can now be written in C.

The control flow constructions that can be used include "if", "while", "do", "switch", "break", "continue",

"return", "goto", etc., so that structured programming is possible. Development of large programs in particular is easier to do if the programming is structured, and the programs are easier to read after they have been written.

When using C it is usual to create a number of functions and then link them into one long program. Therefore, functions which have previously been created and compiled can be re-used. This kind of programming that is done with C, based mainly on functions, leads naturally to the concept of modular programming. A long program is constructed from a number of shorter modules, each on the order of about 50 lines or less. It is much easier to debug short modules than to debug a long program all at once, and the modules can later be re-used in longer programs, greatly reducing the effort required in programming.

The use of C makes it possible to produce high-quality executable programs. High quality means that the execution speed is fast and the amount of memory required is not excessive. It is normal for an assembler program (or machine language program) written specifically for use on certain hardware to be of higher quality, but C is capable of detailed description just like an assembler language, so the result is of nearly the same high quality.

It is difficult and complicated to write a program in a primitive assembler language, but easy in C, which is a high-level language, and since there is not a great deal of difference in the quality of the object program, C is considered to be better to use than an assembler language. However, there is a small amount of software that can only be written in an assembler language. These are the parts of programs that may require the use of certain machine instructions or deal with CPU status flags. Even when assembler is used, however, the specifications are first defined in C, making it easier to later write the program in assembler. This procedure also makes software maintenance easier, and reduces errors, because programmers understand the contents more easily.

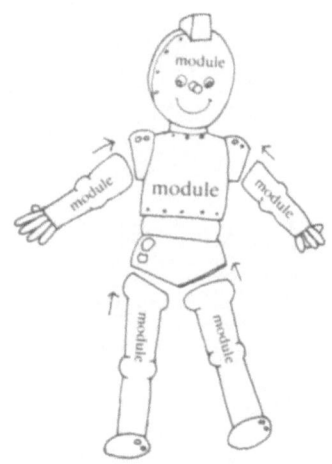

One of the convenient features of C is that long programs can be split up into modules for development

Usually, an assembler language will be available in a form called a macro assembler, which is slightly higher level and easier to use. C is sometimes considered a sort of high-class macro assembler language.

UNIX is written mostly in C, with a small part written in assembler language. The machine dependent part that is written in the assembler language cannot be transferred to other machines, but the part that is written in C can be transferred to any machine that has a C compiler. (However, there are many other programs which are machine dependent and written in C.) The ease of transferring UNIX between many different machines is one of the factors that has led to its widespread use.

Since C is usually used for writing programs to be run on UNIX, C can be used as a common language for communication between users. If someone wants to study the UNIX system, if he knows C and owns a license, he can study the source program for UNIX, since it is written in C. Also, most UNIX utility programs are written in C.

For reasons such as these, the language C is always used when programming on UNIX, thus saving labor in programming.

Example of a program written in C

```
#include <stdio.h>
#include <ctype.h>
#define TRUE    -1
#define FALSE    0
#define WLENG   20
#define itmaloc   ((struct item *) malloc(sizeof(struct item)))

struct item {   char    wd[WLENG];
                int     n;
                struct item *l, *r;
          };
char            wd[WLENG];
struct item     *root;

main(){         /*------------- word count using tree ---------------*/
        struct item     *sift();
        int             i;
        char            c;

        root = NULL;
        do {
                while(((c=getchar())!=EOF) && (! isalpha(c)) && (! isdigit(c)))
                ;       /*------- non alpha-numeric -------*/
                if (c==EOF) treeprint(root) ;
                else {
```

```
                                   i = 0;
                                   wd[i] = c;
                                   while(((c=getchar()) != EOF) &&
                                         (isalpha(c) || isdigit(c))){
                                               if (i==(WLENG-2)) break; /*-too long-*/
                                               i++;
                                               wd[i] = c;
                                   }
                                   i++;
                                   wd[i] = '\0';
                                   root = sift(wd,root); /*----push wd[] into tree----*/
                      }
        } while (c != EOF);
}

struct item  *sift(wd,pitem)
        char             *wd;
        struct item      *pitem;
{

        if (pitem==NULL){
                pitem = itmaloc;    /*--- make new item ---*/
                pitem->n = 1;
                pitem->l = pitem->r = NULL;
                strcpy(pitem->wd, wd);
        }
        else switch (compwd(wd,pitem->wd)){
                case 0 : (pitem->n)++;  break;
                case 1 : pitem->l = sift(wd,pitem->l); break;
                case 2 : pitem->r = sift(wd,pitem->r);
        }

        return(pitem);
}

treeprint(pitem)
        struct item *pitem;
{
        if (pitem->l != NULL) treeprint(pitem->l);
        printf("%20s  %10d\n",pitem->wd,pitem->n);
        if (pitem->r != NULL) treeprint(pitem->r);
}

compwd (w1,w2)
        char  *w1,*w2; /*------- w1[]==w2[]    0---------*/
                       /*------- w1[] <w2[]    1---------*/
        int   i;       /*------- w1[] >w2[]    2---------*/

        for(i=0; i<WLENG; i++){
                if (w1[i]<w2[i]) return(1);
                if (w1[i]>w2[i]) return(2);
                if (w1[i]=='\0') return(0);
        }
}
```

Use of the Editor

Everybody depends on the editor

In using an interactive type operating system, the character strings which comprise the text are input sitting at a terminal and watching a CRT display. Modifications to the input can be made immediately. A program called the **editor** assists this input operation.

The editor inserts and deletes characters into a text. It can also divide a file and merge files. It is extremely useful to both programmers and key punchers.

Since the editor is used by nearly all users, its ease of use has a great effect on work efficiency. If it is easy to use, corrections can be made quickly and work proceeds easily. It not, much time and trouble can be taken editing.

UNIX has a standard editor called **ed**. **ed** edits specified lines, hence is called a line editor. The line to be edited can be designated not only by a number such as 1, 2, 3 ..., but also by its contents; for example, one can designate a line that contains a certain character string. Then commands are given to that line. Not only can a specific sequence of characters be specified, but more general or complex pattern matching functions can be used.

.	one arbitrary character
∧	the start of the line
$	the end of the line
pattern *	0 or more repetitions of the pattern
[. . . . . .]	any single character inside the brackets

For example, [abcde] means any single character from a to e. This can be abbreviated as [a–e]. [A–Z] [a–z] * indicates a character string that starts with a capital letter, followed by zero or more lower case letters; thus, possible character strings include "A", "Abc", "Big", "Tomorrow", etc.

To indicate the three character strings "group1",

"group2", "group3", it is sufficient to write "group.". ^dog ⌣ indicates the character string "dog" starting from the beginning of a line and followed by a blank (_ means a blank).

It is possible that there will be more than one line containing the indicated character string. In such a case the command is applied to all such lines. For example, "dog" can be changed to "cat" wherever it appears in the text. **ed** also contains a number of other features that help to save labor in editing.

In addition to **ed**, there is an editor called **vi** that was developed from **ed** at the University of California at Berkeley. Since **vi** is a full-screen editor, which can perform corrections over the whole screen, it is more efficient than **ed**. The position of the current input is shown on the screen by a cursor. The full-screen editor can move the cursor up, down, right and left so that any character anywhere on the screen can be corrected. Such functions depends on the hardware. However, **vi** has a data base for screen control characters and can be used on nearly any keyboard. Normally, the screen editor is designed for specific hardward and cannot be transferred to other hardware, but **vi** has software that allows the functions of these four keys to be performed by other keys so that it can be used on any hardware.

There are also other advanced screen editors, such as **INed** which is put out by Interactive Systems Inc.

The short command at the right is all that is needed to change "dog" to "cat" wherever "dog" appears in a file. It is convenient to be able to do complicated editing jobs with such short commands

Supervision of Object Program Preparation

A program is normally broken up into several smaller programs which are written, debugged and compiled separately before being linked into a long program. When this linkage is done, and when there are many object programs to be linked, it can become difficult for the user to keep track of which shorter object programs are to be linked and in what order. To help the user keep these things straight, UNIX has a utility program called **make** which updates programs.

make performs the compiling operation and links the smaller programs together in accordance with the instructions in the files. Any one file can be altered without requiring all of the files to be compiled over again. In addition, the machine compares the dates and times when the source program and object program were prepared and, if the source program is newer, re-compiles it to produce a new object program, and re-links it to the other object programs to produce a revised long object program.

This utility makes it easy for the user to maintain supervision over how object programs are made. Also **make** is used, when there are many document files, and only the files which are updated are printed out.

Supervision of Source Programs

Another utility program, similar to **make**, called the **sccs** (Source Code Control System), further extends the usefulness of UNIX as a software development system.

When people start developing programs, it is almost inevitable that a number of versions will result. Since each version is a little bit different than the others, all of them are necessary, but if all of them were to be stored in full

Example of specification of a compilation procedure by MAKE

```
HDR     = as.h func.h code.h inst.h token.h addrmode.h
SRC     = main.c parse.c pseudo.c proc.c jp.c scan.c aout.c data.c
OBJS    = main.o parse.o pseudo.o proc.o jp.o scan.o aout.o data.o
DATA    = instr key

CFLAGS = -UDEBUG -O                    as depends on OBJS, in other
                                       words, on main.o, parse.o,
as: ${OBJS}                            pseudo.o, proc.o, jp.o, scan.o, and
        cc -o as ${OBJS}               data.o

${OBJS}: ${HDR}
data.o: instr key                      In addition, data.o depends on instr
                                       and key
hdr: inst.h code.h token.h addrmode.h

code.h: code.d mkdata
        mkdata < code.d > code.h                   Compiling is done over with this file

inst.h: inst.d mkdata
        mkdata < inst.d > inst.h
                                                   If there is a change in any one of the
                                                   dependent files, compilation is done
token.h: token.d mkdata                            over. Otherwise compiling is not
        mkdata < token.d > token.h                 done over

addrmode.h: addrmode.d mkdata
        mkdata < addrmode.d > addrmode.h

print:
        (list ${HDR} ${SRC} ${DATA} ; (prins | pr -3)) | lpr

type:
        pr ${HDR} ${SRC} ${DATA}

wc:
        wc ${HDR} ${SRC} ${DATA}

rmtmp:
        rm /tmp/as86*

rmobj:
        rm ${OBJS}

save: ${HDR} ${SRC} ${DATA}
        cp ${HDR} ${SRC} ${DATA} savedir
        cp /dev/null save

prins: as
        ln as prins
```

the available disc memory capacity would quickly become filled up. Also, when there are so many versions, if a small change is made in the part that is common to all of them it would have to be made separately in each version, and it is possible that the programmer would forget to change some of the versions. And of course it is necessary to document each version to explain to users what it is and how to use it.

To help with this complicated job of supervising versions of source programs, UNIX has a capability known as **sccs**.

sccs stores only the part of each version that is different from the former, saving a great deal of memory. As changes are made, the changes themselves and explanations of them are inserted in the original files. The changed part is referred to as **delta**. The original files gradually come to contain a number of deltas, but it usually happens that those are small compared to the size of the whole file and do not threaten to overflow the available memory.

When the version that is desired is reproduced, the necessary deltas are operated to the original file, starting from the oldest delta, until the specified version has been reproduced.

The user can make a record of who made each change, where and for what purpose. This information is very valuable in keeping track of all of the different versions.

These differences take the form of editor commands, so that when an original file is edited in accordance with such a command the slightly different version of it is reproduced. This editing can of course be done automatically merely by specifying the file and giving the appropriate command.

Each file is stored together with identification comments telling who prepared it, when and for what purpose.

Original file   Differential file

The complete file can be reproduced by adding the differential file to the original file

Storing a number of nearly identical files in full is wasteful of memory. It is more efficient to store the parts that are different as differential files

Design of User Interfaces

UNIX has special utility programs called **compiler-compilers**, such as **yacc** and **lex**, which are not found in other operating systems. A compiler-compiler is a tool used to produce compilers.

When it is troublesome to write a compiler entirely in C, **yacc** or **lex** can be used to save labor. A compiler consists of three parts, a lexical analysis part, a syntax analysis part (parser), and a code generation part. **yacc** is used to generate the syntax analysis part of the compiler. When the basic syntax analysis rules are given to **yacc**, **yacc** generates the C program which parses words using the method written in these rules. **lex** automatically produces the lexical analysis part of the compiler. Both are very convenient because as soon as the basic conversion rules are input, they output the corresponding program in C.

These are used both to produce computer language compilers and also to design user interfaces. As we have explained earlier in this book, a user interface acts as an intermediary between man and machine. A good user interface makes programs that run on UNIX easier to use.

For example, there are two conversational-type electronic calculator languages, **dc** and **bc**, on UNIX. **dc** is a multi-precision calculator language for which the degree of precision can be set arbitrarily. **bc** is an improved language that is easier to use. **bc** uses **dc** to perform actual calculations, but has the added feature of a user interface so that control flows (such as if, while, and for) can be used, making it easier to use than **dc** by itself. This user interface is written by **yacc**.

When a **bc** command is given, the user interface translates it into a **dc** command and it is then executed as such. The actual calculation is therefore done in **dc**.

Since we can view a user interface as a kind of compiler, it is easier to produce it using a compiler-compiler. The query language **quel** for the data base management system **ingres** is also a kind of user interface. It is also written by **yacc**. Some processing systems that are hard to use by themselves can be made easier to use by adding a user interface.

The compiler-compilers **yacc** and **lex** are tools for producing compilers

CONTROL OF DEVICES

Now let's take a look at how UNIX controls various devices that are connected to the computer. There many types of such devices, including numerically controlled (NC) machine tools such as lathes, CAD/CAM (Computer-Aided Design/Computer-Aided Manufacturing), experimental equipment, and so on. Every control program has to be written separately because its form depends on the machine being controlled. When such programs are written, the superior characteristics of UNIX as a software development system are most useful.

Whenever a new machine is to be controlled by an operating system, one may need to revise the kernel of the operating system. UNIX has the advantage that its kernel is easier to revise than the kernels of other operating systems. This means that it takes less time to hook a new machine up to a computer when UNIX is used as the operating system.

Control of devices often requires **real-time processing**, i.e., as soon as a signal from a peripheral machine is received, the necessary calculations are performed, judgments are made, and results fed back to the machine immediately. Since UNIX is a time-sharing system, it is almost impossible for it to do real-time processing at user program levels. If you need a real-time processing, the modification of device drivers of the kernel is necessary.

On a time-sharing system such as UNIX many users' programs are run, a little at a time, in sequence. After a program runs a little, it can be interrupted to run another user's program. The original program will not run any more until some time has elapsed. Therefore, even if a signal arrives from a machine, it can take time until the user's program realizes that it has arrived and even longer until it is able to issue a response.

It is difficult for a computer to function as a time-sharing system and do real-time processing at the same time. In UNIX, the emphasis is on time-sharing so it does

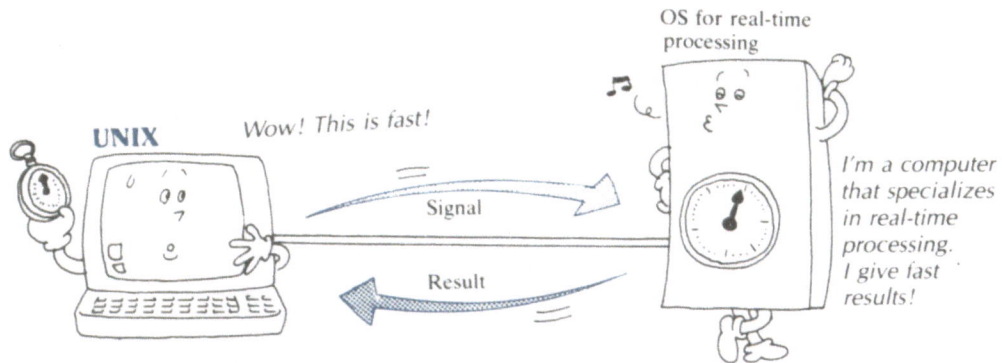

not make a good operating system for real-time processing.

Even so, UNIX is still widely used for controlling machines, and it can do so as long as very high-speed control is not required. UNIX can be used as a software development tool to develop a real-time operating system sharing UNIX's advantages, such as:

· ease of program development
· ease of device interconnection

Chapter 4
Characteristic Features of UNIX

In this chapter we will discuss a number of outstanding characteristic features of UNIX. One of the most important of these is the file concept, which has a considerable influence on the whole system program. In addition, the fact that the files in the aggregate form a tree structure and the fact that there is a command interpreter language shell contribute to providing a user-friendly environment. The abundance of software is itself an important feature of UNIX.

FILE SYSTEM AND ITS HIERARCHICAL TREE STRUCTURE

What Is a File?

We are surrounded by lots of information as we work. Our personal address books, salary data records and records of measurements made during experiments all contain valuable information. We must store such information in a manner that permits us to find it immediately when we need it.

There are many ways to store information. We can, for example, write it in a notebook which will be kept on a shelf, or photograph it on microfilm. In the case of a computer, information is stored magnetically on an auxiliary storage device such as a floppy disc, hard disc or magnetic tape. The information can be anything that can be expressed in the characters that the computer handles: addresses, programs, results of calculations in the form of tables of numbers, and so on.

In a computer, such a collection of characters is called a **file**. This term can refer either to the character string or to the location where it is stored. Each file is given a separate name. The term "file" conjures up an image of a bundle of papers or invoices, but anything consisting of characters can form a file in a computer.

The contents of a file can either be meant to be read by people, or can form an **object file** which is meant to have operations performed on it by the computer. Among the characters stored in files, in addition to human readable characters, there are control characters which are used to control the display on the screen.

UNIX files simply consist of characters, without a troublesome division into blocks and records, so that all files can be handled in a uniform manner. This might sound a little bit abstract, but in UNIX a file is defined as

No matter what the contents, any collection of characters can be a file

"an arbitrary character string".

An arbitrary character string

There are many files on a typical computer disc. The larger the computer system the more files it has, and the harder it becomes to find the file you want when you want it. This makes it important to supervise files carefully all the time.

Different operating systems use different methods of supervising files. One of the principal features of UNIX is the hierarchical structure of its files. Let us now explain what this means.

Hierarchical Structures

UNIX assigns files to a number of different levels for the purpose of supervising them.

"Hierarchy" is a difficult concept to understand. Before we explain what is meant by the "level" of a file, let us take a look at the organization of a company or government department.

For simplicity we assume that the organization of a certain company is very simple and straightforward. A single President heads the company. Below him are several heads and below each division head there are several department heads. Each department head has a number of ordinary employees as his subordinates. Thus, this company is organized into groups of employee ranked in the order **company → division → department**. This is a kind of hierarchy, and it clarifies the position of each employee within the company. If you specify "Mr. A in Department B of Division C of Company D", then, unless of course there are two people of the same name in the same department, you have identified that person uniquely.

From the point of view of a supervisor, this kind of hierarchical organization makes it easier to supervise the company. The division of labor and the purpose of each division and department is clear.

A hierarchical tree structure

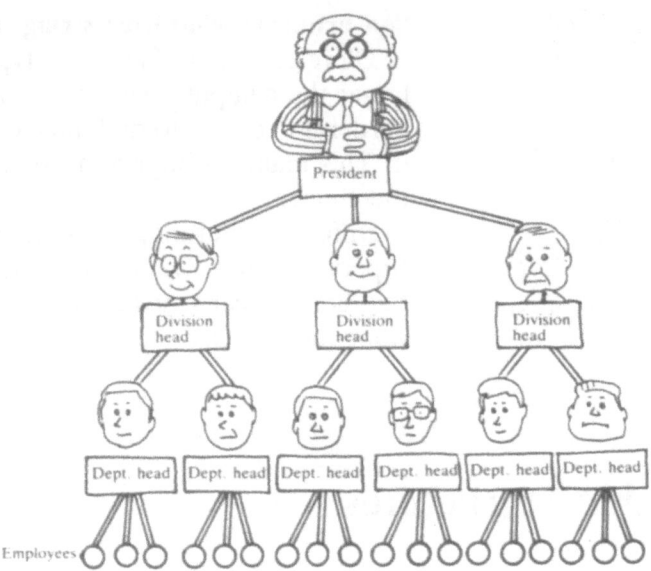

Several division heads below the president form, in a sense, several branches radiating out from a single point, or apex. Each division head, in turn, looks like an apex from within his division, and from him several more branches, representing the department, radiate. Then below each department head are the individual employees. This kind of branching structure is called a **tree structure**. A tree branches out from a single base at the top of its root system, and forms a number of **nodes** from which branches radiate. In general, in a tree structure, the number of branches at each node and also the numbers of descendant levels at each node can be decided freely.

This kind of structure is called a **hierarchical tree structure**. Just as in the case of personnel supervision in a company, files in a computer are easier to supervise when they are organized into this kind of structure. One of the principal features of UNIX is its organization of files into a hierarchical tree structure. Compared to operating systems which do not have this kind of structure, this structure saves a good deal of labor in various kinds of operations and gives UNIX a number of advantages, such as the ease of supervising files. Recently, a number of

"UNIX-like" operating systems, which also have hierarchical tree structures, have appeared.

In a multi-user system such as UNIX there are many files in it, and it is necessary to keep each user's files separate. This is easy to do if the user creates all of his files under his own node. If the user generates a large number of files, he may group his files by creating more than one node for himself.

File Structure of UNIX

All of the files in UNIX are organized into a single overall structure, much as the branches of a tree all come from a single root. A place where branches split off is called a node. The branches correspond to files. A node is itself a kind of file, but it is different from an ordinary file. We cannot store any arbitrary character string in it. It is, rather, a mechanism for file supervision, called a **directory**. The directory contains a couple listing of all files and directories hanging from it. In the broadest sense the term "file" includes directories, but for simplicity in the following discussion we will use the term "file" to refer only to ordinary files in which arbitrary character strings can be stored, and a file that is used for supervision will be called a "directory".

This "tree" can also be represented as a kind of genealogical relationship, with the patriarch at the apex replacing the tree root. Seen from his position, the directories immediately below him are directories of his children. On the other hand, seen from some generation, the directories just above it are directories of parents. Thus, directories link files in what is called a **parent-child** relationship. Looking at the system from some file within it, a file of a "preceding generation" is said to be on a "higher level", and a file of a "succeeding generation" is said to be on a "lower level". The directories and files that are linked to a given file and on higher levels than it are

There are three kinds of files

File {
  Directory
  Ordinary file
  Special file*
}

*Special file: refer to "Special Input/Output Files" in this chapter

UNIX family tree

collectively said to be its "**ancestors**", while those on lower levels are said to be its "**descendants**".

If we start at a certain file and progress to successively higher levels from it, we eventually come to the directory on the uppermost level, from where we cannot go to any higher levels. Thus this directory corresponds to the president of a company or the roots of a tree. In UNIX this directory is called the **root** of the system.

If we draw a diagram of the whole system with the root at the top, there will in general be several directories and files hanging down from it and several other directories and files hanging down from each of directories. An ordinary file cannot have other files or directories hanging down from it. "Children" can only be produced at a location where branching takes place, in other words, at a directory. However, a directory can have both files and directories hanging down from it.

Madam Directory

The information in a directory concerns only its own children. It does not contain information about descendants further down the line

Just as each employee, department and division in a company has a name, each file and directory has a name. This name is given to each file or directory at the time it is created. A directory contains the name of each file and directory below it, and the position in which each file and directory is located. Therefore, by creating a file, under a certain directory an actual file entity is related to a file name. Each directory contains only the name of its immediate "children"; it does not contain the names of any files on still lower levels in the hierarchy. Of course, two or more children of a certain parent cannot be given the same name, but children of different parents can be given the same name.

Directories for Users

As soon as a user starts to use the UNIX system, he is given a directory. For the moment we need not worry about the ancestors of that file, and can concentrate on the problem of how to create its descendants. At the beginning there are no files under this directory. Only when the user starts to use the directory does it come to have files under it. As more and more files are created, the directory comes to have more and more children. However, the contents of the files can differ greatly from one file to another. It could become confusing if we had, for example, document files for document creation, program files containing programs under development, and various kinds of data files all mixed together on the same directory. To help create some order out of chaos, it is usual to create one directory for one purpose, and then "hang" related files and directories below it. Dividing all directories up into document creation directories, program development directories and data directories, and keeping these groups separate, makes the system easy to use. This can be compared to creating project teams within a company department to clarify the role of each individual employee.

● Directory
○ Ordinary file

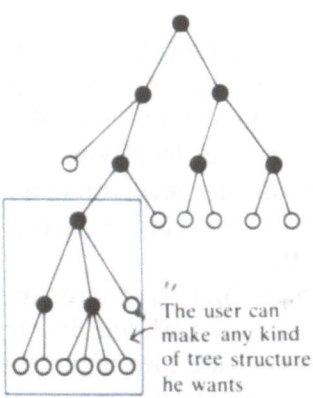

The user can make any kind of tree structure he wants

The user's directory

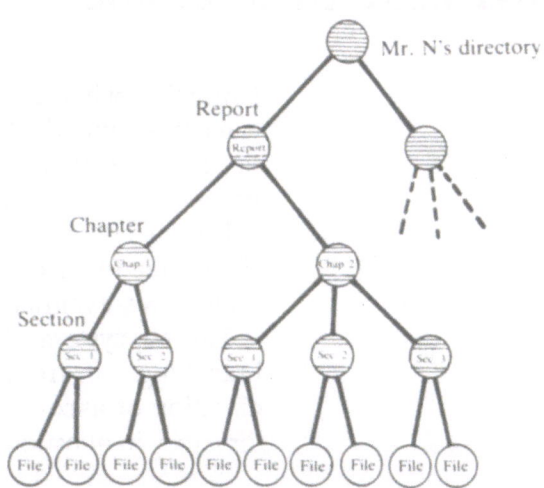

Thus, the user can supervise files in such a way as to make his own work easier, by creating files and directories under directories. A number of levels of directories can be created, making a variety of different methods of organization possible. For example, if a long document is to be stored in files, it would be convenient to create several levels of directories, corresponding to the whole report, chapters and sections. Then files containing the actual text sections would be hung down from the section directories. The directory for Chapter XX has directories for all of the sections in that chapter below it, each section directory in turn has a number of files. This is a good example of a hierarchical tree structure.

In a file system which does not have a tree structure, the files are all lined up in a row and the system does not know the relationships between them, so the user must keep track of those relationships. In UNIX, with its hierarchical tree structure, the relationships between files are easier to understand than in other operating systems. It is also possible to save labor by such means as specifying all of the descendants of some file and performing some operation on them.

Transfer between Directories

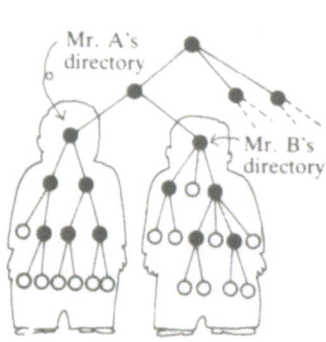

Normally, when a user works on a certain directory, he can access only the "children" that are directly connected to that directory. To access a "grandchild" file, it is necessary to transfer to a directory one level lower.

It is also possible to transfer to a higher level directory. If transfer to successively higher level directories is continued, we eventually arrive at the root.

The file system of UNIX forms a single tree structure branching off from the root. As we proceed in the direction of ancestors, the contents of the files under the directory in question have broader and broader impact, so that the damage done by a mistake in manipulating the directory increases at higher levels. At a very high level, an error could even damage UNIX itself. Such high level files are usually made inaccessible except to specially authorized people.

A number of prepared files are provided as part of UNIX. They are the control program for the operating system, the utility programs which execute UNIX commands, the application programs for users, and so on. It can also happen that there are descendant files of another user's directory which one would like to use.

In order to access these various files, we must first transfer to the parent directory that has both the current file and the desired file as descendants and then transfer back down another branch until the desired file is reached. With the exception of some files which have been deliberately made inaccessible (as explained above), the user can transfer to any directory in the big branching tree that forms the UNIX file system. And the user can access his own files and even to other people's files.

The idea of treating files as a kind of shared property is not new, but there have been numerous difficulties in actually doing this with previous operating systems. The freedom that UNIX gives the user to transfer from one

A user can move from one directory to another and then use the "child" files of each directory. But there are some directories that can't be accessed

file to another throughout the system makes it possible to use other users' files. This has resulted in a great increase of sharing of programs among users and also in using existing programs as parts of new programs.

Of course, there is still the problem that you can't use someone else's program if you don't know how to use it. UNIX alone can't solve this problem. But at least UNIX provides an environment which makes sharing easier. Meanwhile, UNIX carefully guards those files which the owner wants to protect.

Protection of Files

UNIX makes it easy to use others' files, but it also provides **protection functions** for files which you don't want other people to see, to alter or to execute.

For example, if a company develops a program which it wants to keep secret, it is necessary to protect that program from being read by anybody outside of the project team that is developing it. There are also documents which must be kept secret. Data in a salary file must be protected from being rewritten without authorization. And it is necessary to protect programs under development from clumsy tampering by beginners, and to protect programs and files from malicious alteration by somebody possessing evil intent.

It even sometimes happens that you want to protect some of your programs from being executed by other departments within the same company.

To meet these requirements, UNIX permits access to each file and directory to be limited with respect to the following permission modes for different classes of users:

Read   Write   Execute
These three authorizations are possible for each file

1. Read   (r)
2. Write   (w)
3. Execute   (x)

These operations have slightly different meanings when applied to files as opposed to directories. Without permission to read a file, you can't see what is in it. Without permission to write in a file, you can't alter it. And of course being able to execute a file depends on having permission to do so.[1]

Read permission for a directory determines whether or not it will be possible to obtain a list of the "child" files and directories of that directory. If read is prohibited, the list cannot be obtained, but there is no effect on access. Therefore it is still not prohibited to transfer to child directories or alter them.

Write permission is needed to create a new "child" below a directory or to destroy an existing one.

When execution of a directory is prohibited, it becomes impossible to access any of its descendants. However, it is possible to obtain a list and to see the children. These three permissions can be granted independently of one another. Permissions can be granted to any of the following groups of users:

1. The owner of the file or directory
   (the person who created it).
2. User group.
3. Other users.

1 The only files which can be meaningfully executed are compiled object programs and shell procedures

Let us now explain what is meant by a group. In the example of a project team given above, the development of the program cannot proceed unless members of the team have **r**, **w**, and **x** permissions. But it is necessary to keep people outside the team from having access to the file. UNIX permits a group to be defined by registering the names of the people who belong to it. In this example the owner and his group would be given all three authorizations, and other people would not be given any.

What kind of permission is given for a file or directory, and to whom it is given, together comprise what is called the **protection mode**. The protection mode can only be changed by the user who created the file or directory, called the owner, and by the system supervisor who is called a **super user**. Since the super user is responsible for the operation of the system, he has a number of special rights that ordinary users do not have. However, in the case of a very important secret file, it is possible that you will not want even the super user to know what is in it. UNIX provides the capability to put the contents of such a file into code that the super user cannot understand. Only a person who holds the keyword to the code can decode it.

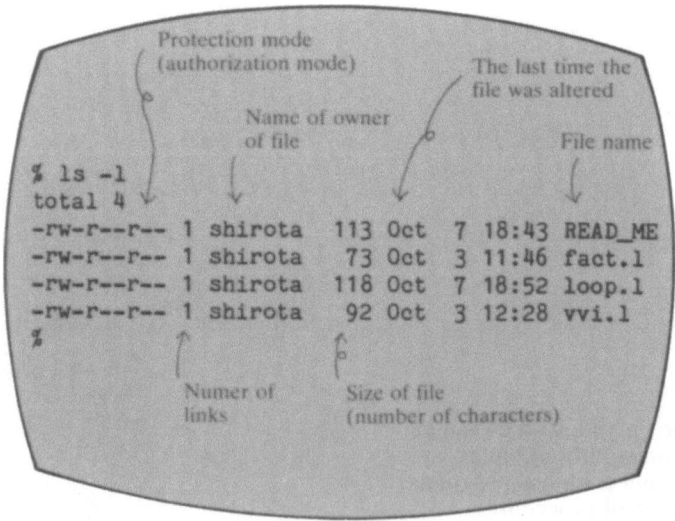

Detailed display of the contents of a file (or directory) on the screen using the command **ls -l**

Protection modes (authorization modes) of files

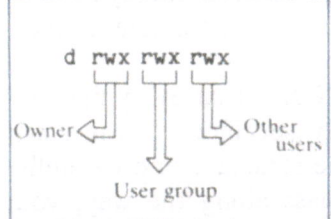

```
% cd games
% ls -l
total 1867
-rwxr-xr-x 1 daemon        54 Apr  3  1984 aardvark
-rwxr-xr-x 1 daemon     35860 Feb 12  1982 adventure
drwxr-xr-x 2 daemon        48 Sep 21 16:44 advfiles
-rwx--x--x 1 root       20986 Mar  2  1983 aliens
-rwxr-xr-x 1 daemon      5264 Feb 12  1979 arithmetic
-rwxr-xr-x 1 daemon     16384 Oct 16  1980 backgammon
-rwxr-xr-x 1 daemon     15340 Oct 16  1984 banner
-rwxr-xr-x 1 daemon      2816 Oct 21  1979 bcd
-rw-r--r-- 1 daemon    256977 Mar 28  1982 bogdict
-rwxr-xr-x 1 daemon     17408 Oct 16  1980 boggle
-rwxr-xr-x 1 oct        33662 Feb  3  1982 canfield
-rwxr-xr-x 1 root       21504 Dec 20  1984 chase
-rwxr-xr-x 1 daemon      4136 Oct 16  1983 chess
-rwxr-xr-x 1 daemon       168 Dec 18  1981 ching
-rw-r--r-- 1 root       23552 Sep 21 16:58 core
-rwxr-xr-x 1 root       20480 Nov 10  1984 cribbage
-rwxr-xr-x 1 root       24276 Jul  9  1981 doctor
-rwxr-xr-x 1 daemon     11264 Oct 16  1980 fish
-rwx--x--x 1 78          9116 Mar  6  1983 fortune
```

This is an ordinary file. Since the owner has **rxw** authorizaiton, he can do anything, but other people are only allowed to execute (x)

"-" (a hyphen) indicates no permission. "d" indicates a directory; if "d" is replaced by "-", then the file is an ordinary file

Coding and decoding file by CRYPT

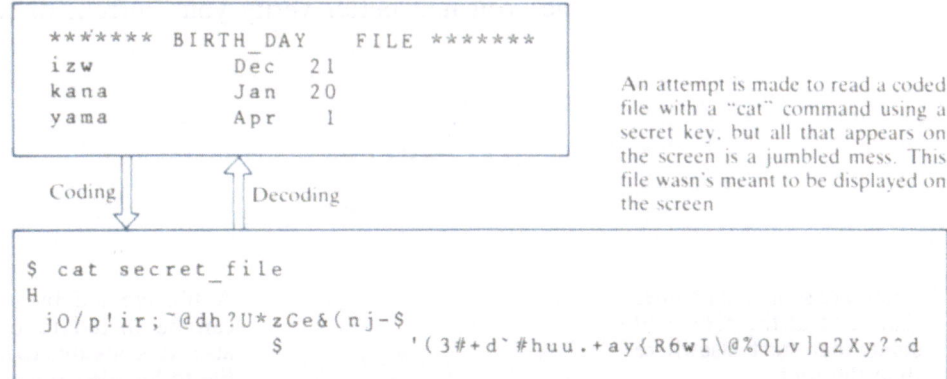

Original file

```
****** BIRTH_DAY   FILE ******
izw        Dec  21
kana       Jan  20
yama       Apr   1
```

Coding / Decoding

An attempt is made to read a coded file with a "cat" command using a secret key, but all that appears on the screen is a jumbled mess. This file wasn't meant to be displayed on the screen

```
$ cat secret_file
H
 jO/p!ir;~@dh?U*zGe&(nj-$
         $           '(3#+d`#huu.+ay{R6wI\@%QLv]q2Xy?^d
```

Uniqueness of Files by Path Names

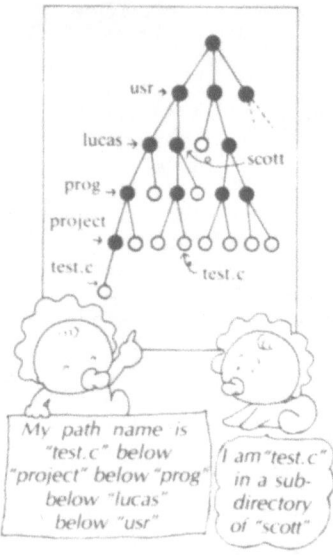

My path name is
"test.c" below
"project" below "prog"
below "lucas"
below "usr"

I am "test.c"
in a sub-
directory
of "scott"

UNIX has many users. Suppose that you and another user create different files but give them the same name. Will the system mix them up? The answer is NO. This is because even though the two files have the same name, they belong to different parent directories. This is similar to being able to distinguish two children who have the same first name because they have different family names. Even if the family name is the same, it is possible to trace their ancestry to determine who's who.

A characteristic feature of UNIX is that every file and every directory can be uniquely specified. If you start from the root of the UNIX tree structure and carefully specify which directories you pass along the way, you naturally arrive at only one file. In UNIX, the collection of directories that you pass through in order to get to a certain file (or directory) is called a **path**. Each file is given a **path name** which uniquely specifies the directories that you must pass through, starting from the root, in order to get to it.[1]

Therefore, even if two users give different files the same name, if you see the whole path name you can immediately tell that they are different. However, in UNIX, since the user switches freely between directories as he uses the system, occasionally he will lose track of which directory he is at, and access a different file of the same name as the one he wants. Before you use any command to update a file, you had better verify your current directory.

1 There are some path names that start at the root, and some that start elsewhere than the root

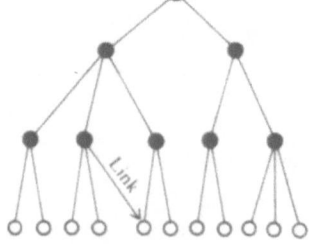

A file created by somebody else can be linked to one's own file also. It is possible to link one's own file to his file, too.

To enstate another user's file as a child file of one's own directory as well is called **to link**. After linking is done, the user can use the file as though it were in his own directory, but it is not the same as having copied the file to create a new file. The file still exists in only one place.

Special Input/Output Files

Let us consider the calculation of salaries in a company. Two existing files are needed: one that contains the program that does the calculation, and one that contains the data to be used. The data file contains information about company employees. A third file will be necessary to store the results of the calculation. First data are taken out of the data file, then the actual calculation is performed, and finally the results are output to an output file.

Thus, there are times when input files and output files are necessary. In such a case it is necessary to specify an input/output file name. What happens if an output file is not specified? The results of the calculation will still be displayed on the screen of the terminal. If, on the other hand, an output file is specified, the results will go into that file and not be displayed.

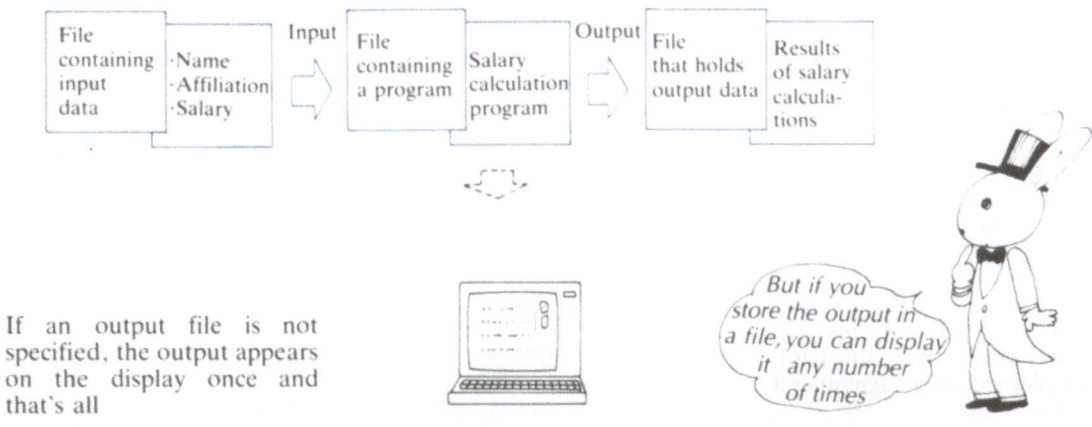

| File containing input data | ·Name
·Affiliation
·Salary | Input | File containing a program | Salary calculation program | Output | File that holds output data | Results of salary calcula-tions |

If an output file is not specified, the output appears on the display once and that's all

But if you store the output in a file, you can display it any number of times

The keyboard can be thought of as a kind of input file

It would seem that a display is really a kind of file. But there is a difference. You can send data to the display, but the computer can't take them back out. If the display tube is turned off, those data are lost. We can think of a regular file as having a "basket" at the bottom, while a display has a "hole at the bottom" so that character strings just pass through and never return.

So, then, what about the keyboard, which is the standard input device? A keyboard is used for input of character strings, but it can still be regarded as a file. A printer is also regarded as a special file.

Thus, all input and output devices such as the display, keyboard and printer can be considered as a kind of file, called a "**special file**" in using UNIX. They have their own file names and can be specified just like a regular file when input or output is to be performed. This is very convenient to the user in writing a program. It is not necessary to follow a special procedure just because it is input or output. Being able to treat input and output devices just like other files lightens the burden on the user.

In UNIX, if nothing at all is specified then the keyboard is regarded as the input file and the display is regarded as the output file. These are called the "standard input" and "standard output".

When results of a program are being output, the CRT display can be thought of as a kind of file

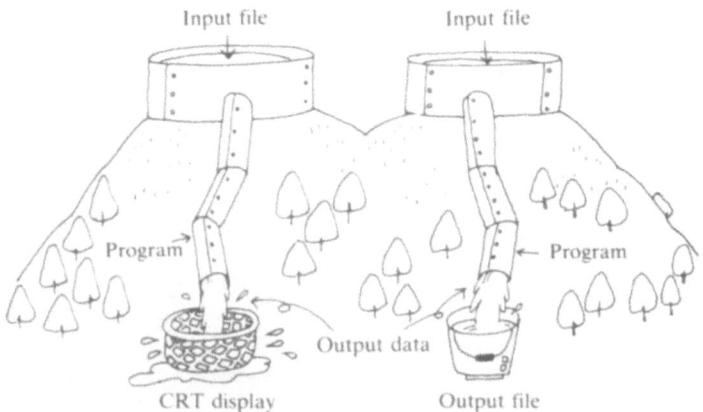

Input to and Output from Files

In UNIX, special input/output files can be treated just like regular files. For example, in order to display the content of a file called "**test**" using a file print command **pr**, the statement **pr test** would be used. If it is also desired to store the data in another file called "**junk**", the statement would become **pr test > junk**. This causes a copy of the result of **pr test** to be entered into **junk**. Since it has been specified that the flow of data which had been going to the CRT is now to be directed to **junk**, all of the data are now in **junk**. If it is instead desired to print the data out on a printer, all that is necessary is to write the file name of the printer in place of "**junk**". For example, if the file name of the printer is "/dev/sp0", then the statement becomes **pr test > /dev/sp0**. Since the format of commands stays the same for all files, even special input/output files can be handled easily.

> **pr test** .... display on the CRT display, which is the standard output device
>
> **pr test > junk** .... output to file "junk"
>
> **pr test > /dev/sp0** .... output to printer

Seen from the point of view of UNIX, this is the same as changing the standard output file. When nothing is specified the output goes to the CRT display; ">" redirects the flow of data as indicated.

Similarly, "<" is used to switch from the standard input device (the keyboard) to another input device.

> **cat < test** .... input from file "test"

Special files have file names, just like ordinary files

Files Used to Run UNIX

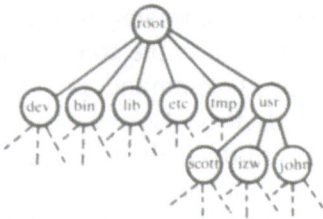

The standard children of the root in the UNIX file system

The entire file system of UNIX forms a single tree structure. Depending on the particular system, there is a variety of individual files and directories that make up the tree, but the basic files and directories needed to run UNIX remain more or less the same. Let us look at what kinds of basic directories are needed.

Immediately under the root of the tree structure, the following directories are attached as "children". Then the remainder of the file system is descendants of these directories.

dev
bin
lib
etc
tmp
usr

Let us now explain the characteristics of each of these directories.

dev (device)
The various special files are usually grouped under this directory.[1] In UNIX input/output devices such as printers, keyboard, CRT display, plotters, etc. are regarded as special files, so each of these devices has its own file name and becomes a descendant of **dev**. In addition, the file names of external memory devices such as hard discs, floppy discs and magnetic tape units also have file names which go here. Because each UNIX system has its own devices, the descendants of **dev** differ greatly from one system to another.

bin (binary)
The directory called **bin** has files containing executable utility programs as its descendants. These programs can be executed immediately upon receipt of the appropriate

1 UNIX allows these files to be anywhere; it is only by convention and for convenience that they are grouped into the /**dev** directory

UNIX command. When the user inputs such a command from the keyboard, the program in the corresponding command program file, which will be a descendant of **bin**, is executed immediately.

lib (library)
Files that "hang" from **lib** contain subroutine files that are used by the library programs and the utility programs. The computer language processing systems will be found here. For example, part of the C compiler is here.

etc (et cetera)
Data used by the UNIX system and utility programs which must not be tampered with are contained in files under this directory, as are files which are used for maintenance of the system. Also, the file in which the names of all users of the system are registered is here.

tmp (temporary)
Temporary files come under this directory. For example, a file which contains an intermediate version of a text which is being edited would be a descendant of **tmp**. Since all files here are temporary and are accessed very frequently, a medium which can be accessed quickly (such as a hard disc) is normally used to store them.

usr (user)
This directory is for the purpose of creating more directories underneath itself. Since there are many files and directories which are descendants of this file, they are often stored on secondary memory devices which can be disconnected. The standard input/output subroutines for C programs are found here.

Among the directories which are "children" of **usr**, we find some with names **bin** and **lib**, which have already appeared as directory names above. This is because the secondary memory is sometimes not big enough to hold all of the descendants of those directories. In such a case, it is necessary to hold part of **bin** and **lib** on portable memory volumes which can be disconnected.

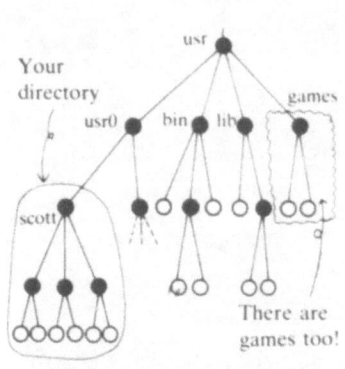

An example of the possible arrangement of descendants of **usr**

There is also a directory called **games** which has games such as backgammon, chess, checkers, hangman and so on under it. The ability to include such fun games in the system is one of the interesting features of UNIX, for which we can thank the designers of UNIX at the Bell Telephone Laboratories.

Finally, all of the directories created by ordinary users go under **usr**. The system supervisor can consider what kind of system would make the work in his research institute or company proceed most smoothly, and design a hierarchical structure for user files that will best suit those requirements.

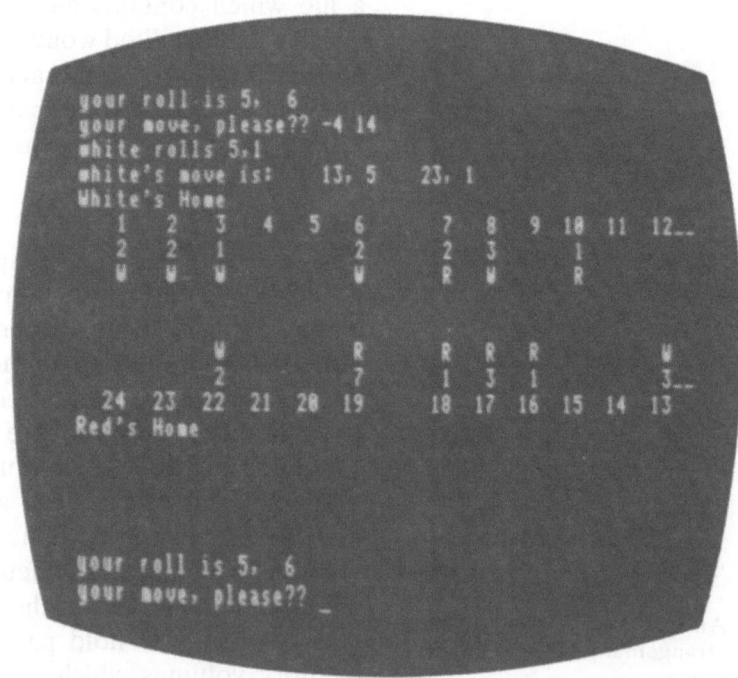

An example of a screen display during a game of backgammon

COMMAND PROCESSING LANGUAGE SHELL

Command Processing System

People who operate a computer have many tasks to perform. They must create new files, delete files which are no longer needed, look at what is in files, merge files or split them up, compare two files to see what is different about them, and so on. They must perform basic operations such as compiling programs and specifying input and output files to be used in the execution of those programs.

These basic operations affect all people who use the computer whether they are programmers or typists who are using the computer as a word processor. From the point of view of effective use of human resources, a system which requires operators to be working on it all of the time so that the real work can never progress, or a system on which it is easy for the operators to make many errors, is wasteful.

What parts of an operating system determine whether it will be easy to use or not? Actually the answer is not easy; it depends to a great extent on the quality of the software which executes commands which are input by people. A **command** must be given to get the computer to do anything, whether to perform a file operation, to compile a program, or to do anything else.

The command system of UNIX is designed to improve the operator's efficiency

One problem is what kind of commands there are in the system. A system of commands which represents the various operations simply and clearly is a great help to the operators. If you want to create a good environment for computer operation, one of the first things to do is to select an operating system which includes a command processing system that will increase the working efficiency of the operators.

The UNIX Command Processing System: Shell

UNIX has a command processing system that is very easy to use. It is called **shell**. We will gradually describe the numerous outstanding features of shell, but first let us take a basic look at its capabilities.

As soon as a user sits in front of a terminal and starts to use UNIX, a shell program starts to run for that user. Then the computer goes into a state of readiness to receive a command from the user (or operator). When the operator inputs a command at the keyboard, that command is immediately input into shell.

The work that shell performs is "to convert commands that are easy for a human being to understand into a command that can be understood by the machine". Shell analyzes the character string that forms a command. Once it understands the name of the command, it searches for the file of that name, and then executes the command. In many cases, the command file will be under **/bin** or **/usr/bin**. Shell also deciphers the argument or arguments which often (although not always) follow a command and when necessary, redirects the flow of data from/to standard input/output files.

Thus, shell can be referred to as what is called a **command language interpreter**.

Shell bridges the gap between the operator and the computer to provide an operating environment that is comfortable for the operator. When the user starts to operate that computer, that user's own exclusive shell starts to run to create an environment that is suited to him. When many users are using the computer, at least that many (usually more) shells are running to interpret the commands input by the different users.

The standard command files provided with UNIX are under the **/bin** and **/usr/bin** directories, but a user can also create a directory for his own command files. In UNIX, regardless of where a file is stored, if it has an attribute of "executable" its contents can be executed as a command (we sometimes speak of executing a file rather than executing a command). When a command is input,

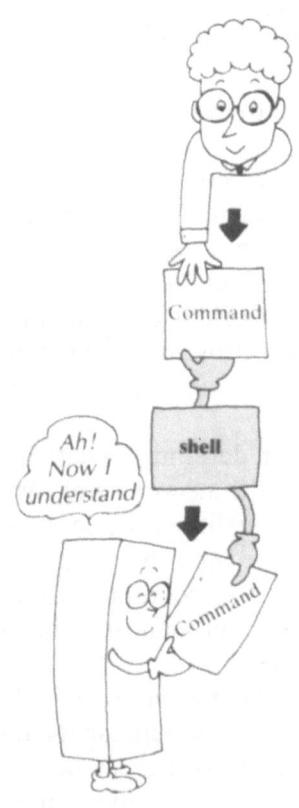

"Shell" is a command language interpreter, which interprets the commands which people input to the computer

the shell searches the directories in the **specified path** in sequence. A shell variable **PATH** indicates the search sequence and the value of **PATH**. The following is an example of a **PATH**.

PATH = :/usr/superman/bin :/bin :/usr/bin

- The null character string (nothing at all) just after = indicates the current directory.

When a command **ls** is executed by shell in the above example, at first shell tests the existence of **ls** in the current directory. If it does not exist, shell tests the existence of **/usr/superman/bin/ls** and so on. This command search path can be varied from one user to another.

Simple Clear Commands

UNIX is an operating system which puts out few messages

In order to perform operations using UNIX, one must learn the commands provided for use with the shell. The command names are simple. Also, there are very few messages output from the shell; in fact there are very few messages output from the shell; in fact, there are almost none except when there is an error in the input. For an experienced operator, simple commands and few messages make it very easy to work. Since an experienced operator will not make many mistakes, fewer messages means fewer interruptions. In this sense the system is designed for experienced people. Since UNIX does not usually output many messages, there is little that one can do except to assume that it is working correctly.

However, this simplicity can make the system hard for a beginner to use. A beginner tends to make many mistakes. The simplicity of the commands means that the damage done by one mistake is multiplied, and the lack of messages means that the beginner often isn't quite sure of what he is doing and becomes uneasy.

But, if the beginner is conscientious and pays attention to what he is doing, the simplicity of the processing system can actually help him to progress faster. And once he does get used to it, he will come to appreciate the simplicity.

Definition of Commands

The user can easily create his own command file

There are certain sequences of operations that recur over and over again in the work of a computer operator. It is convenient if such a sequence of operations is combined into a single command.

The shell has the capability to allow each user to define his own commands. A file that holds such commands is called a **command file**. If such a command file is created and then marked as executable, the user has made a command that he can use privately.[1]

Once such a command has been created, the trouble of inputting long command sequences each time through a keyboard is eliminated, increasing the efficiency of the work. Such a grouping of several commands is called a **command procedure** or **shell procedure**.

Also, within the shell, variables called **shell variables** can be used. Long character strings are often used as values of shell variables. If a long character string is used as a shell variable, it then becomes unnecessary to repeatedly input a long string.

A shell variable can be used within a shell procedure. Its value can be given later by a command argument.

Some shell variables are used to set a user's environment. Their examples are **PATH** (explained above), and **HOME**. **HOME** sets a user's home directory. The values of them can be changed by the user freely.

1 To make a file usable as a command it is sufficient to give execution (**x**) as that file's protection mode

Wild Card Characters

In order to make it unnecessary to input all file names in full at the time of file specification, what are called "wild card" characters can be used in the file names. (Editor's note: This name comes from certain card games, where special cards can be used to stand for any card at all that the player wishes.) There are the following three types of wild card characters.

*	Any arbitrary character string including the null string (the character sting of length 0 characters, in other words, nothing)
?	Any one arbitrary character
[...]	Any one of the characters between the brackets

Let us now try to make use of the **ls** command which all child file names and directory names. We now have child files such as the following. If "d*" is specified, it could

```
% ls
data1_1      data3_1      prog.c      t         test78.c
data1_2      data3_2      prog.o      temp
data2        data3_3      prog.s      test
```

mean any of the six file names that start with "d" (here we mean "file" in the broad sense). It is, in fact, shell that does the work of replacing "d*" by the following six file names.

```
% ls d*
data1_1      data1_2      data2      data3_1      data3_2
data3_3
```

If "prog.?" is input,

```
% ls prog.?
prog.c  prog.o  prog.s
```

appears; if "data?_?" is input,

```
% ls data?_?
data1_1      data1_2      data3_1      data3_2      data3_3
```

appears while if "*" is input,

```
% ls *
data1_1      data1_2      data2        data3_1      data3_2
data3_3      prog.c       prog.o       prog.s       t
temp         test         test78.c
```

appears. The combination of [13] with * and ? gives:

```
% ls *[13]??
data1_1      data1_2      data3_1      data3_2      data3_3
```

Also, abbreviated forms can be used in the brackets; [a–z], [0–9] indicate any lower case letter from a to z and any digit from 0 to 9, respectively.

Wild card characters can be used in combination, and can be used in any arbitrary location, in front of, in the middle of or after a character string.

Shell Procedures

This is just like a program, isn't it!

In a shell procedure, just as in a high-level programming language, it is possible to write a program using such commands as "**for**", "**case**", "**while**" and "**if**". In order to be able to use such control flow constructions, it is necessary to acquire some programming experience with a language such as C, PASCAL, etc.

It is often convenient to use shell procedures when instructing the computer to perform certain processing. It is of course possible to write a program entirely in a programming language such as C or PASCAL, but this can sometimes be unnecessarily troublesome.

What is the difference in using a shell procedure? A shell procedure has a number of tools called UNIX commands. Therefore it is not necessary to start from the beginning each time as when writing a computer program.

Example of a shell procedure

```
        if     test $# -le 0
        then
               echo "Usage: gar c [-p] [-r recordsize] name ..."
               echo "    or gar x [-p] [-]"
               echo "    or gar t [-p] [-]"
               exit
        fi
        case $1 in
        c)
               shift
               /usr/lib/arc $@;;
        t)
               shift
               /usr/lib/tab $@;;
        x)
               shift
               /usr/lib/ext $@;;
        *)
               echo "Key must be c, t or x.";;
        esac
```

syntax of if ~ then ~ fi

syntax of case ~ esac

Instead, it is only necessary to combine existing commands. The simpler the commands provided with a shell, the easier it is to combine them to perform a complicated operation.

Since it is easier to create a shell procedure than to write a complete program, the time devoted to programming is reduced. Also, minor modifications of existing commands become easy by using shell procedures. Since a shell is an interpreter, it will not let you wait like compilers. While you talk to it, things are done and ready.

Data Flow and Pipes

Many UNIX commands are of such a form that a character string is input from an input file and the result of the processing done by that command is output to an output file. Let us now return to the subject of the flow of data and pipes, which was discussed briefly in Chapter 3. In a typical command (which is really a kind of program) data flow in from the standard input device, the command causes that flow of data to be processed in some way, and another flow of data which is obtained as a result of the processing is output to the standard output device. According to this way of thinking, the flow of data that takes place when a command is executed somehow resembles the flow of water in a pipe.

As long as other input and output files are not specified, the standard input and output devices (special files), namely, the keyboard and the CRT display (or teletypewriter), are assigned as the input and output files. Consequently, one input file and one output file are always used in the execution of a command.

Thus, in the execution of a command there is a single flow of input data (generally the standard input) and a single flow of output data (generally the standard output), and the data flow much like water. Such a command with the standard input and output is called a **filter**. This way of thinking about the flow of data is not peculiar to shell commands; it is general for all of UNIX. However, the flow of data is different from the flow of water. Once water flows out it is gone, but in the case of data they are really only a copy of the contents of the input file that flows out, and the same data remain in the file.

When a number of shell commands are executed in sequence, there are invisible files called **pipes** which combine output and input functions. A pipe takes the data from the standard output flow from one command and, without sending the data to an output file, causes the same data to become the standard input flow for the next command. This is an interesting name, reminding us of the pipes used to transport a flow of water.

A pipe is designated by a vertical bar: "|"

Suppose we wish to take data from an input file called **data**, execute a command called **tst**, **sort** the results and then output them to a file called **result**. Without using a pipe, we would have to write the following:

```
tst < data > temp
sort < temp > result
```

First the output from the command called **tst** is stored in a temporary file called **temp**; then the contents of **temp** are used input for the command **sort**. After that there is the need for an additional operation to delete the file **temp**.

If on the other hand we use a pipe, we need write only the following:

```
tst < data | sort > result
```

The pipe makes it unnecessary to specify an output file or input file in the middle of the program, resulting in great simplification.

Now let us use pipes in a somewhat more complicated operation.

Input data

For one command program, there is one flow of input data and one flow of output data

Command program

Output data

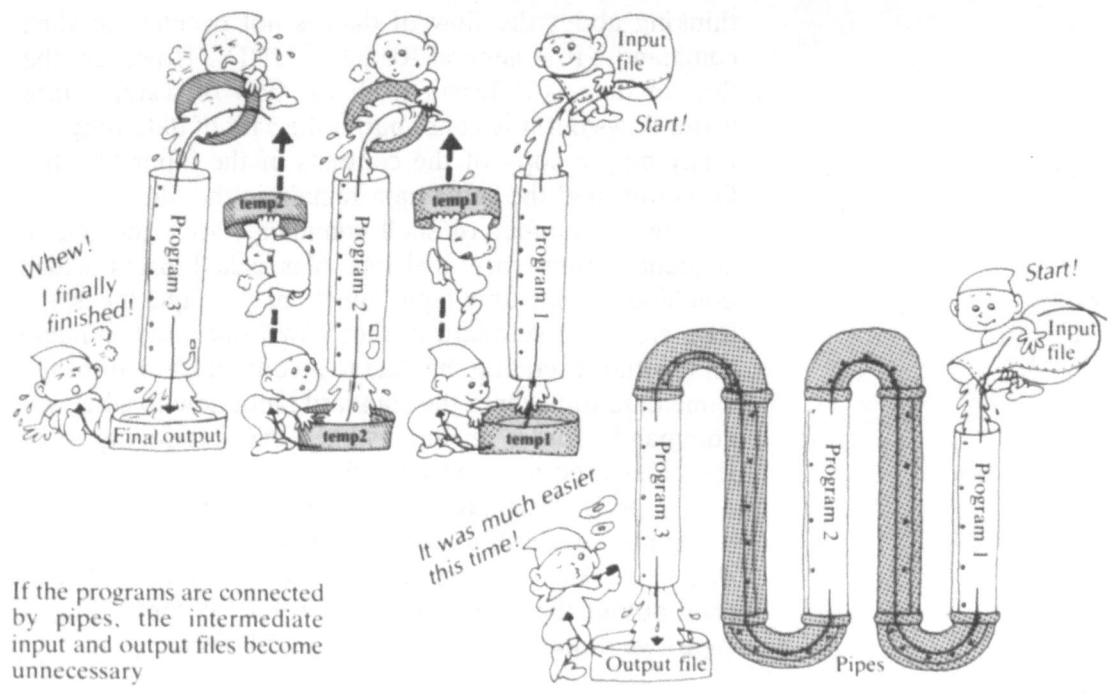

If the programs are connected by pipes, the intermediate input and output files become unnecessary

Example 1:

Suppose that we are mailing letters to all of the people whose names are stored in a file called **name1** and also to all of the people whose names are stored in a file called **name2**, and wish to make sure that two letters are not mailed to the same person. The desired list can be produced by combining **name1** and **name2**, sorting the entire combined file and then eliminating duplicate lines. The commands which are used are the following.

cat: Concatenates two or more files.

sort: Sorts the contents of a file.

uniq: Eliminates duplicate lines which follow each other in succession, leaving only one in place of two.

Let us now combine these commands with pipes:

cat name1 name2 | sort |uniq

This pipe concept is a characteristic feature of shell, and hence of UNIX.

Example of processing using pipes
(combination of two lists of names)

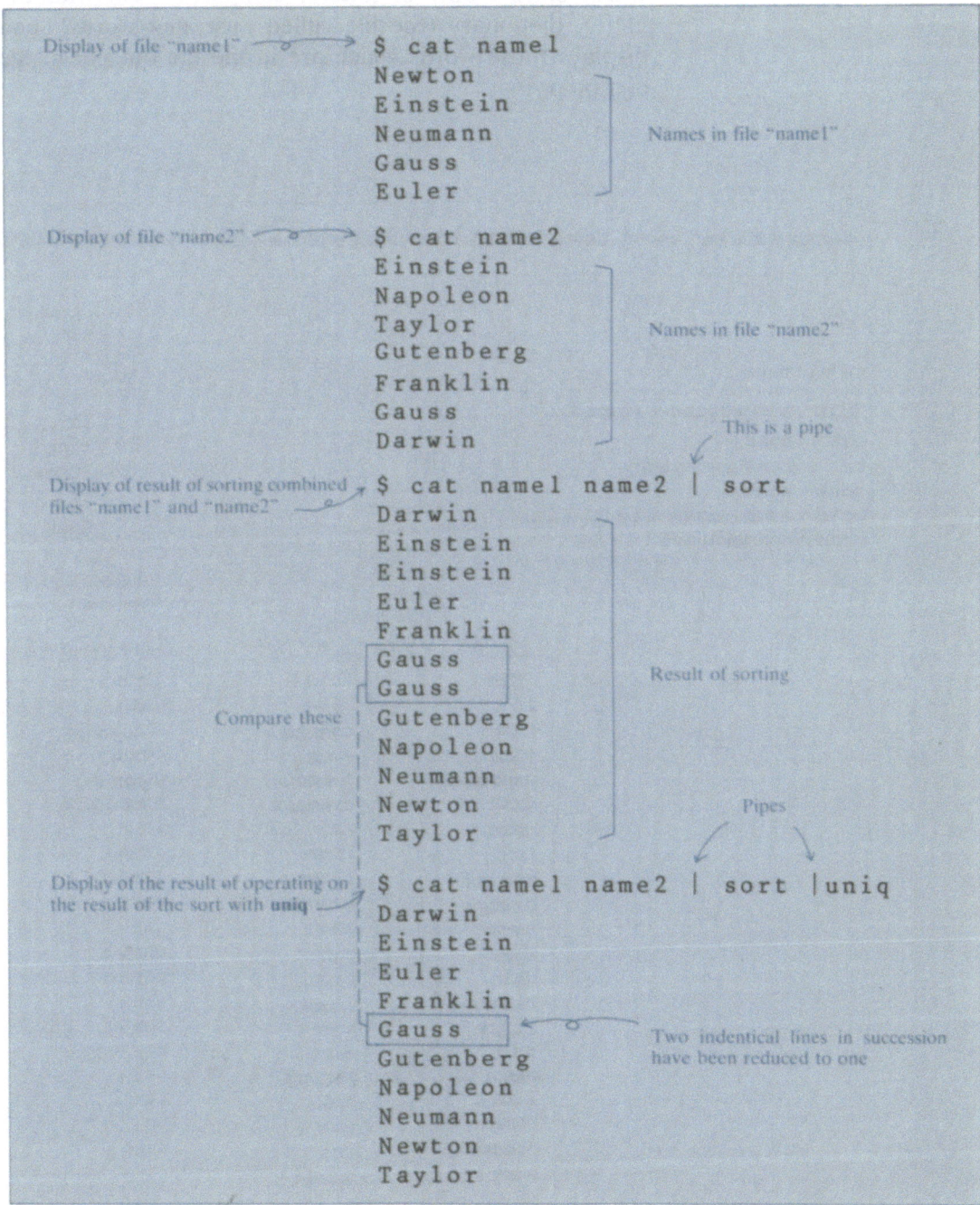

Example 2:

This program selects all of the words in a specified file whicn consist only of letters, compares them with the UNIX dictionary (the file called **/usr/dict/words**), and displays those words which are in the file but not in the dictionary:

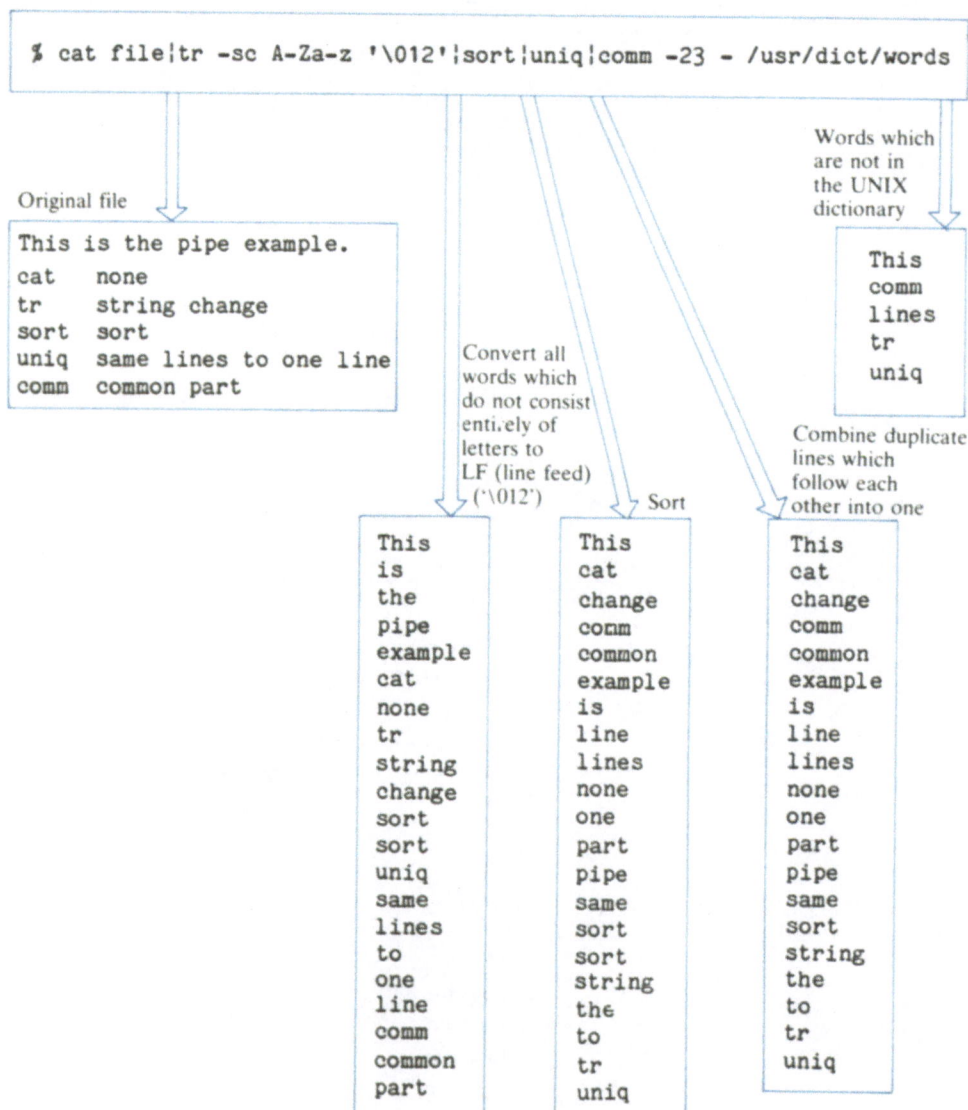

```
% cat file|tr -sc A-Za-z '\012'|sort|uniq|comm -23 - /usr/dict/words
```

Original file

```
This is the pipe example.
cat    none
tr     string change
sort   sort
uniq   same lines to one line
comm   common part
```

Convert all words which do not consist entirely of letters to LF (line feed) ('\012')

Sort

Words which are not in the UNIX dictionary

```
This
comm
lines
tr
uniq
```

Combine duplicate lines which follow each other into one

```
This        This        This
is          cat         cat
the         change      change
pipe        comm        comm
example     common      common
cat         example     example
none        is          is
tr          line        line
string      lines       lines
change      none        none
sort        one         one
sort        part        part
uniq        pipe        pipe
same        same        same
lines       sort        sort
to          sort        string
one         string      the
line        the         to
comm        to          tr
common      tr          uniq
part        uniq
```

Background Jobs

It is possible for an operator to become impatient while waiting for a command which requires a long processing time, such as the compilation of a program, to finish. If one user has a number of programs to run, then it is convenient if those programs which require a long processing time can be kept running somewhere "out of sight" while the user runs other programs, such as file editing, at the same time. Such parallel running of jobs reduces wasted time and speeds work.

UNIX permits one user to run a number of jobs at the same time. This is called a **multi-programming system**. Those jobs which are running where the user "cannot see them" are called **background jobs**. UNIX permits a number of background jobs to be run at once. This multi-programming capability, which permits a single user to run a number of jobs at once, is an important feature of UNIX. Such time-sharing processing (or TSS) greatly increases the efficiency of a conversational-type operating system. However, the user must use caution because if the number of jobs becomes too great the processing speed will be slowed considerably.

UNIX is a superior operating system developed and improved through the years at the AT&T Bell Laboratories

AN ABUNDANCE OF SOFTWARE

Software Environment of UNIX

The most important thing a user wants to know about any operating system is what kind of software will run on it. We have already seen that UNIX provides an abundance of software. Examples are the computer language, tools which aid software development, utility programs and application programs.

Since the source code of UNIX itself, written in C, has been made available to licensees, many users added new capabilities to the system. This is itself a cause of the great abundance of software available for UNIX. UNIX is now used by many users around the world, including many users in universities, government agencies and private companies, particularly software companies. As users of UNIX increase in number, they add more software, which makes UNIX still more useful, causing the number of users to increase further. This self-reinforcing cycle has resulted in both very widespread use of UNIX and in a great abundance of software for the system.

The simple CP/M operating system has become standard for use on 8-bit microcomputers, and a great deal of software runs on it, but it appears as though UNIX will become the standard operating system for 16-bit microcomputers. UNIX is also running on many minicomputers and main frame computers. Having many computers use the same operating system has the great advantage for users that once they have mastered that one system, many computers become accessible to them. Another advantage is that the user may have many colleagues who use the same operating system.

UNIX has still another important difference from other operating systems. This is the superiority of UNIX as a

UNIX has lots of software!

software development system. Software developers like to use UNIX because it provides an easy-to-use environment for program development.

Even when the UNIX system was first developed at the Bell Telephone Laboratories, that development was itself done on UNIX. Improvements to and maintenance of UNIX were done on UNIX. When a system is used for system development, it must be used in ways different from the way it is ordinarily used, and the way of using it often pushes the limits of the computer system. Therefore, the fact that UNIX has been successfully used for development of itself attests to what a highly refined, easy-to-use operating system it is.

Therefore, many software companies, which must live or die on their ability to keep creating and selling new application programs and utility programs, rely heavily on UNIX. This is a good thing for all UNIX users, since professional software developers normally create much more new software than other users.

Now let us take a more detailed look at just what kinds of commands are available for UNIX. Since there is too much to describe here, we will limit our discussion to the important and generally applicable software. Most of the software listed below can be executed in the form of commands; thus, all that is necessary to execute a program is to input the name of the file in which that program is stored.

Control of User Access

LOGIN (log in)
Whenever a user sits down at a terminal and starts to use the computer he must first run this program, which supervises the start of his use of the computer. The user inputs his **login name** at the keyboard. The first thing the computer does is to check whether that name is listed on

that particular file, in other words, whether that user is entitled to use the computer. If not, then he cannot use it. To prevent another person from logging in somebody else's name and thus gaining unauthorized access to the computer, each user can have a secret **password**. The password is not displayed on the CRT display of the terminal when keyed-in, making it difficult for an unauthorized person to learn it.

Then, if electronic mail has arrived for the user, a message that there is mail is displayed. Using a mail command, the user can freely decide whether to read the mail or not and whether to erase it or leave it stored in memory.

Next, the UNIX system displays various messages. For example, in the morning it might say "good morning" or in the afternoon, "good afternoon", followed by "How are you?" or "Have you eaten lunch?". Perhaps such a greeting makes UNIX seem like a more "friendly" system to some users.

At the same time as **login**, another file called ".**profile**", which is set up by the user, is automatically executed. One of the functions of **login** is to execute this file. The execution of ".**profile**" sets up the appropriate environment for each user. For example, some users might want

What a login looks like

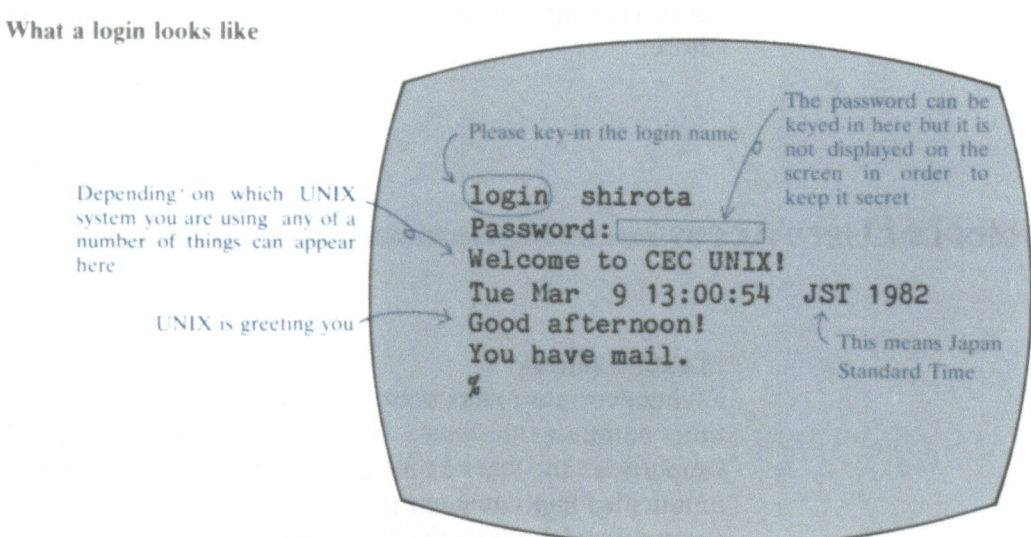

Depending on which UNIX system you are using any of a number of things can appear here

UNIX is greeting you

Please key-in the login name

The password can be keyed in here but it is not displayed on the screen in order to keep it secret

login shirota
Password:
Welcome to CEC UNIX!
Tue Mar 9 13:00:54 JST 1982
Good afternoon!
You have mail.
%

This means Japan Standard Time

to execute the word processor program immediately following display of the date. In such a case, a command to do just that would be included in ".**profile**". Then as soon as the user logs in, the word processor will be set up and ready to use.

In other words, ".**profile**" becomes an input file for certain input which would otherwise have to be keyed in on the keyboard. This provides a suitable, personalized working environment for each user as soon as the user logs in. If the user is a beginner, then the system supervisor can set up a working environment suitable for beginners. An inexperienced user is not forced to start using shell commands from the beginning. Rather, a command menu system can be used to provide an easy-to-use shell at the beginning. Also, since many beginners are wasteful of CPU time, it is often limited.

People who use UNIX only to key in data can have an appropriate environment for that set up as soon as they log in. Thus, the system supervisor is able to suitably simplify the operating environment for inexperienced users. This permits beginners to progress rapidly without being confused by the complexity of the total system.

After ".**profile**" is executed, a user's shell commands are executed.

Still another function of **login** is to connect a user to his own current directory, which must be done at log in time.

To summarize, the principal functions of **login** are:

- Input and check of the user's name and password
- Updating the accounting files
- Establish working directory
- Display of contents of **/etc/motd** (message of to-day) which are information from the super user (for example, "Welcome to CEC UNIX!", etc.)
- Setting up the user group
- Setting up the environment (for example, **path**, **form**, etc.)
- Activation of the user's shell

An environment with restrictions can be provided for a beginner

PASSWD (password)
This program sets up and alters passwords.

NEWGRP (new group)
This changes the user group, and, for security, verifies the group password.

Handling of Files

UNIX contains all of the programs necessary for such operations on files as combining files, splitting files into two or more files, output of files, copying of files, etc. There are programs used for output to the printer; some of these programs do not merely output the file but add a title and the date to each page, add page numbers, output each page in a number of separate columns, etc. There is a program called **cmp** (compare) which compares two files to see if they are identical, a program called **dd** which copies files from one device to another such as discs and magnetic tapes, and so on.

In addition, there are programs which are specially designed to operate on the hierarchical tree structure file system of UNIX. Examples of these are **mkdir** (make directory), which creates new directories; **rmdir** (remove directory), which deletes directories which are no longer necessary; **rm** (remove), which removes both a file name and its contents; **cd** (change directory), which permits transfer among directories in the tree structure; and so on.

LN (link)
A program to establish a relationship between an existing file and a directory so that the file is treated as a child of that directory is called **link**. This program links files to directories. Linking permits a user to use a file created by another user as a child of his own directory. Linking differs from copying in that there is still only one file, but

there are more names by which that file can be specified. This capability is convenient when two people are working together to improve a file.

This program is perhaps most widely used when many people are to use a certain file without writing anything new in it. Since complete use of files is made possible by linking, it has become wasteful for people to insist on having separate copies of files for themselves.

CHMOD (change mode)

Each file has three possible **protection modes**, read, write and execute, and each protection mode can be applied to three classes of users: the owner, the user group, and other users.

chmod is a program which is used to change the protection mode. It can only be used by the owner of the file and by the super user.

chmod can be used for directories as well as files.

FIND (find)

This program searches among the tree structure of UNIX for a file that satisfies a certain condition, and then performs specified processing on that file.

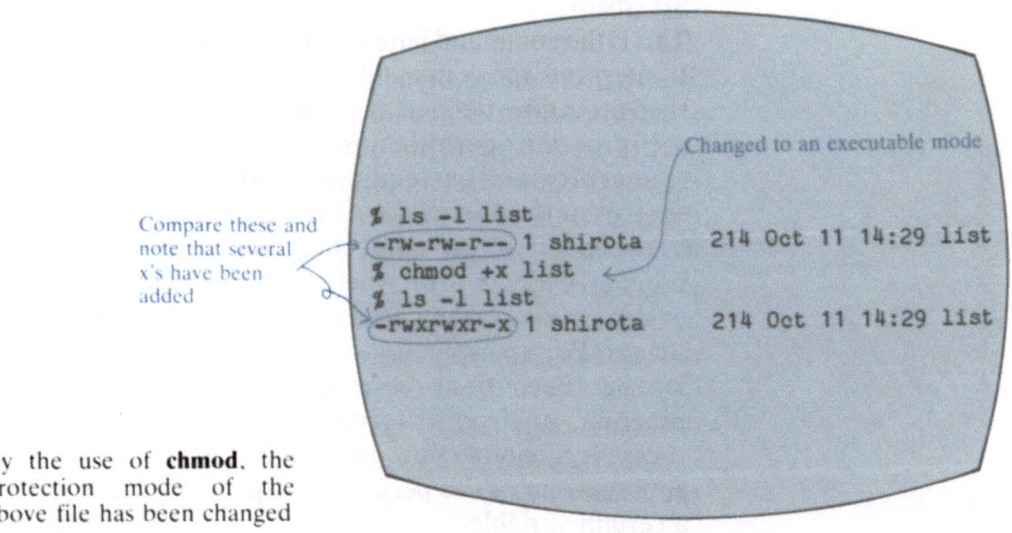

Changed to an executable mode

Compare these and note that several x's have been added

```
% ls -l list
-rw-rw-r-- 1 shirota        214 Oct 11 14:29 list
% chmod +x list
% ls -l list
-rwxrwxr-x 1 shirota        214 Oct 11 14:29 list
```

By the use of **chmod**, the protection mode of the above file has been changed

Since the system supervisor frequently performs such operations as display of all of the files created on a certain specified date, **find** is a valuable program to have. It is even possible to list all files whose names fit a certain pattern.

There are many types of conditions which can be used to specify the file to be searched for, and these conditions can be combined. Some examples:

- Name of file (It is sufficient to specify only a pattern rather than the whole name.)
- Whether the file being searched for is an ordinary file or directory
- How many places the file is linked to
- Owner's name/group name
- Size of the file
- How many days since the file was last accessed
- How many days since the file was last altered
- A file that was altered after some other specified file

Execution of Programs

SH (shell)
This is the command language processing system program. It interprets the commands input from a terminal and the shell procedure defined by **the user**, and then executes it. A shell procedure performs just as complicated processing as a regular program, but requires only a fraction of the effort on the part of the user. Since a shell procedure can possess an **if** command it can alter the flow of processing of a program depending on whether a certain file exists or not, or depending on the outcome of comparison of character strings. For example, it can judge whether or not compiling has been done correctly, and if so, execute the program, or if not, it gives an error indication.

case is a control flow construction which causes different processing to be performed depending on the value of a certain variable.

The shell procedure can also use such control flows as **while**, which causes certain processing to be repeated until a specified condition is satisfied, and **until**, and **for** loops, which also cause processing to be repeated.

EXPR (expression)

This program evaluates arguments as an expression. Such an expression can include combinations of arithmetic operators and relational operators.

AT (at)

Since UNIX has an internal clock, an arbitrary time can be specified and a program executed at that time. **at** has many conceivable interesting applications. For example, a programmer who is staying overnight at his place of work in order to work late can leave a message to be awakened at a certain hour. That message will then be automatically displayed on the terminal, so that someone else can see it and wake the programmer up. The computer can also inform all users that the computer will shut off by message a certain minutes before the power is actually shut off.

Status Reports

There are a number of programs which inform the user of the current status of UNIX. For example, the names of all of the "child" files of a specified directory can be displayed followed by the status of each file (size, owner's name, last date on which altered, last date on which accessed, protection mode, etc.). There is also a program which can inform the user of who is using the computer at present and what kind of processing is in progress.

A user can also inquire as to, for example, who he is (log-in name), what date is today, at what position in the tree structure is the directory presently being accessed, and so on.

"ls" command   An **ls** command causes all of the child files of the specified directory to be listed

```
% ls -l
total 4
-rw-r--r-- 1 shirota        113 Oct  7 18:43 READ_ME
-rw-r--r-- 1 shirota         73 Oct  3 11:46 fact.1
-rw-r--r-- 1 shirota        118 Oct  7 18:52 loop.1
-rw-r--r-- 1 shirota         92 Oct  3 12:28 vvi.1
%
```

"date" command   A **date** command causes the current date and time to be displayed

```
% date
Tue Oct 11 15:01:47 JST 1983
%
```

"who am i" command   With this command you can find out what your login name is

```
% who am i ←   What is my login name
shirota        (I forgot it)?
%
```

"who" command   All of the users presently using the computer are listed

```
        ←   Who is using the computer now?
% who
kana        console Jan  3 14:38
izw         ttyb0   Jan  3 14:37
inaba       ttyb1   Jan  3 11:48
tomo        ttyb3   Jan  3 14:10
%
User's name   Name of terminal   Time of login
```

"pwd" command

```
% pwd
/usr/usr1/shirota
%
```

This command requests the computer to inform you what directory you are at. The answer shown here means the directory called "shirota" which is a child of the directory "usr1" which is a child of the directory "usr" which is below the root. The first "/" indicates the root; subsequent "/" marks indicate partitions

"ps" command

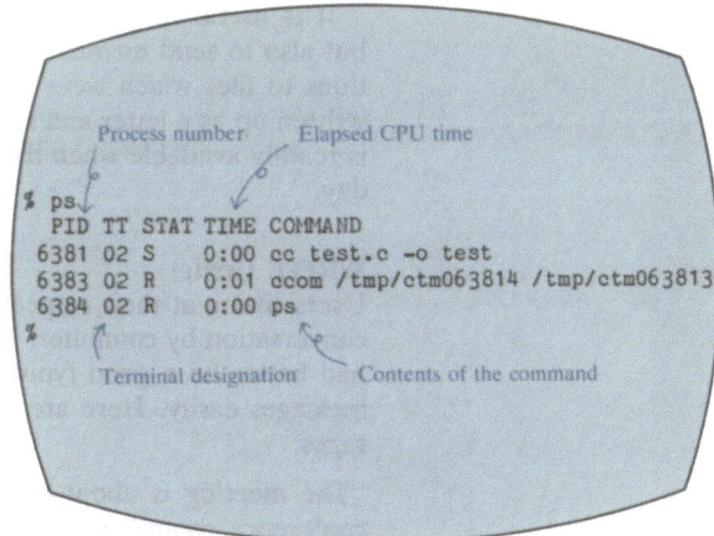

Process number   Elapsed CPU time

```
% ps
  PID TT STAT TIME COMMAND
  6381 02 S    0:00 cc test.c -o test
  6383 02 R    0:01 ccom /tmp/ctm063814 /tmp/ctm063813
  6384 02 R    0:00 ps
%
```

Terminal designation   Contents of the command

The **ps** command requests the computer to inform you of what processes are presently under way

AC and SA (accounting and shell accounting)
ac is a program which provides cumulative statistics on which users are using the computer and how much each of them has been using it. **sa** is a program which provides statistics on which commands are being used and how much each one is being used. Such reports can provide a good overall picture of how the computer is being used. These programs are used mainly be the system supervisor.

Communication

MAIL (mail)
This program handles the electronic mail function of UNIX. A message or letter is input from a terminal or a file. It can be sent to several people at once. Every time a user logs in he is informed of whether mail for him has arrived. Letters can either be stored in files or erased.

It is useful to not only send letters to other people, but also to send memos to oneself. For example, alterations to files which were made on a certain day can be written up as a letter and stored, so that this information is readily available when the user resumes work the next day.

WRITE (write)

Users sitting at their respective terminals can carry on a conversation by computer. To send long messages a user had better be a good typist, but anyone can send short messages easily. Here are some examples of such messages:

"The meeting is about to start so please come to the conference room."
"I will be delayed so please go without me."
"It's noon. Let's go to lunch."

The system supervisor can use a program called **wall** (write all) to send identical messages to all users. For example, he can notify them all to stop using the computer temporarily during the computer maintenance time.

However, it sometimes happens that the person to whom such a message is sent is busy and cannot engage in conversation. In such a case a conversation between the two people is impossible. There is also a program that a user who doesn't want to be bothered can use to prevent **write** messages from coming in.

CALENDAR (calendar)

This program informs a user of his schedule for today and tomorrow, assuming of course that these have been input previously. For people whose work is closely tied to the computer, this is sometimes more convenient than writing the schedule on paper.

UUCP (UNIX to UNIX file copy)

Two UNIX systems running on two different computers can exchange files. A user can copy a file from another computer, or have one of his own files printed out on

uucp permits one UNIX system to copy another's files

another system. This makes for effective use of hardware and software resources. A telephone call is placed from one UNIX system to another; the communication then proceeds over the telephone line. The calling is done automatically by a device called the "automatic calling unit". Of course, a direct communication line can also be used where one exists. Since the communication is between two UNIX systems, it is possible to not only transmit files, but also to execute commands on the other system by remote control. A **uux** (UNIX to UNIX command execution) does this.

The **cal** command causes the calendar of any month of any year to be displayed

```
                                    1985

            Jan                      Feb                      Mar
   S  M Tu  W Th  F  S      S  M Tu  W Th  F  S      S  M Tu  W Th  F  S
         1  2  3  4  5                     1  2                     1  2
   6  7  8  9 10 11 12      3  4  5  6  7  8  9      3  4  5  6  7  8  9
  13 14 15 16 17 18 19     10 11 12 13 14 15 16     10 11 12 13 14 15 16
  20 21 22 23 24 25 26     17 18 19 20 21 22 23     17 18 19 20 21 22 23
  27 28 29 30 31           24 25 26 27 28           24 25 26 27 28 29 30
                                                    31

            Apr                      May                      Jun
   S  M Tu  W Th  F  S      S  M Tu  W Th  F  S      S  M Tu  W Th  F  S
      1  2  3  4  5  6               1  2  3  4                           1
   7  8  9 10 11 12 13      5  6  7  8  9 10 11      2  3  4  5  6  7  8
  14 15 16 17 18 19 20     12 13 14 15 16 17 18      9 10 11 12 13 14 15
  21 22 23 24 25 26 27     19 20 21 22 23 24 25     16 17 18 19 20 21 22
  28 29 30                 26 27 28 29 30 31         23 24 25 26 27 28 29
                                                    30

            Jul                      Aug                      Sep
   S  M Tu  W Th  F  S      S  M Tu  W Th  F  S      S  M Tu  W Th  F  S
      1  2  3  4  5  6                  1  2  3      1  2  3  4  5  6  7
   7  8  9 10 11 12 13      4  5  6  7  8  9 10      8  9 10 11 12 13 14
  14 15 16 17 18 19 20     11 12 13 14 15 16 17     15 16 17 18 19 20 21
  21 22 23 24 25 26 27     18 19 20 21 22 23 24     22 23 24 25 26 27 28
  28 29 30 31              25 26 27 28 29 30 31     29 30

            Oct                      Nov                      Dec
   S  M Tu  W Th  F  S      S  M Tu  W Th  F  S      S  M Tu  W Th  F  S
         1  2  3  4  5                     1  2      1  2  3  4  5  6  7
   6  7  8  9 10 11 12      3  4  5  6  7  8  9      8  9 10 11 12 13 14
  13 14 15 16 17 18 19     10 11 12 13 14 15 16     15 16 17 18 19 20 21
  20 21 22 23 24 25 26     17 18 19 20 21 22 23     22 23 24 25 26 27 28
  27 28 29 30 31           24 25 26 27 28 29 30     29 30 31
```

This broadens the range of files and data bases that one system can use. Besides transmission of files and remote execution of commands, mail can also be exchanged between UNIX systems, thus broadening the group of users with whom electronic mail can be exchanged.

cu (call UNIX) permits a remote terminal to get in on the communication between UNIX systems. A terminal connected to one UNIX system can input a command to a second UNIX system or obtain output from the second system. In other words, a user can make use of the remote system as if he were sitting at a terminal connected to it. This is called a remote terminal capability. The first UNIX system, to which the terminal is primarily connected, need not necessarily do any more than supervise the sending and receiving of input and output to and from the second system.

Computer Languages

C
C is a high-level language which makes structured programming possible. Almost all of the UNIX software is written in C. Programmers who wish to make improvements to UNIX must learn C so that they can read the source code and write the necessary revisions. To use UNIX it is generally sufficient to know only C.

C program tools with UNIX include **cc** (C compiler), **lint** (a C program verifier), **cb** (C program beautifier), and **sdb** (C program symbolic debugger).

LINT
A characteristic of the C language is that programs can be developed in small modules which are later combined. Since the modules are compiled separately, it occasionally happens that they do not match correctly.

lint is a program which checks programs written in C; mainly it checks to see how well the different modules are matched. **cc** also checks for errors, but the checks performed by **lint** are stricter and more detailed, so that it is a good idea to use **lint** whenever it is difficult to determine the cause of an error.

CB (C beautifier)

cb makes a C program neat-looking and easy to read. This not only makes the program look better, but also makes it easier to find bugs.

FORTRAN

Compilers available for FORTRAN include the **f77** compiler, which has the capabilities of ANSI (American National Standards Institute) FORTRAN 77, and **ratfor**, which permits structured programming to be done with FORTRAN.

BASIC

There is an interpreter called **bas** which resembles BASIC. In comparison to the regular BASIC, it has been expanded to permit **recursive** functions to be defined.

DC and BC

Both of these are conversational type calculator languages, which permit the computer to be used like a desk-top calculator. They can be set to perform calculations accurate to any desired number of digits, and input/output can be done in either decimal, binary, octal or hexadecimal numbers. **bc** is a somewhat high-level version of **dc**; whenever a program in **bc** is executed, **dc** is called.

M4

This is a global macro processor. Its main function is the substitution of character strings, similar to "#define" of C and "define" of RATFOR.

YACC and LEX
These are systems used to create compilers. These are not normally needed by an ordinary programmer, but software developers are thankful for these compiler-compilers. One must only give the conversion rules, and the C program which has the functions corresponding to these rules is automatically produced. **yacc** and **lex** are not available with other operating systems, and their availability is one of the principal advantages of UNIX as a software development system.

Program Development Tools

UNIX includes various types of library packages, programs for maintaining them, assemblers and debuggers, loaders, dump programs and other program development tools.

Basic Library Package
This is packaged as a set of subroutines and can be used freely when creating software. It includes a library of mathematical functions including trigonometric functions, a random number generator, a memory area allocation capability, standard input/output package, and so on.

PROF (profile)
This is used when one needs to know what part of a C program is using the most computer time. **prof** reports the number of times each subroutine is called and the amount of computer time it takes.

MAKE (make)
When a number of programs are linked into a single long program, as changes are made in the various component programs, one sometimes loses track of which ones

Example of a program written by YACC

```
/*  mkt_get.y --- parse routine 'mkt' command.
 *       History: Aug 25, 1983; Nobuhiro Ajitomi
 */
%{
#include <sccs.h>
#include <stdio.h>
#include <ctype.h>
#include "mkt_def.h"
#include "toddef.h"

SCCSID(@(#)mkt_get.y      3.10     8/31/83 12:38:30)
static char      user0[STRLNG + 1], mesg0[STRLNG + 1];
%}

%token NUM       NAME     STRING  WDAY

%%
tod_file:        /* null */
        |        tod_file tod_def;
tod_def :        sharp interval time day user mesg {
                         gen_code();
                         fprintf(outfile, ",\n");
                 } ;
sharp    :       /* null */ {
                         sharp = 0;
                 }
         | ';' {
                         sharp = 1;
                 }
         ;
interval:        /* null */ {
                         interval = ONEDAY;
                 }
         | '(' NUM ')' {
                         interval = $2;
                 }
         | '(' '-' NUM ')' {
                         interval = -$3;
                 }
         ;
time     :       '*' {
                         clear_time();
```

Only part of this sample
program is shown

Example of a program written by LEX[1]

```
%{
/*----- insymbol part of PASCAL-S's compiler ----*/
int    i;
main(){
        while(yylex()>0) ;
}
%}
NONAL                   [^a-z0-9]
%%
[ \t\n]*                                         ;
"(*"([^*];"*"[^)])*"*)"                           ;
(
(and|array|begin|case)    |
(const|div|downto|do)     |
(else|end|for|function)   |
(if|mod|not|of|or)        |
(procedure|program)       |
(record|repeat|then|to)   |
(type|until|var|while)  )/{NONAL}
                                printf("%ssy\n",yytext);
[a-z][a-z0-9]*                  printf("ident %s\n",yytext);
[0-9]+"."[0-9]*                 printf("realcon %s\n",yytext);
[0-9]+                          printf("intcon %s\n",yytext);
":="                            printf("becomes\n");
"<="                            printf("leq\n");
"<>"                            printf("neq\n");
">="                            printf("geq\n");
".."                            printf(":\n");
"'"."'"\[^']                    printf("charcon %c\n",yytext[1]);
"'"'"\[^']                      printf("charcon NULL\n");
"'"([^']|"''")*"'"            { printf("string ");
                                yyleng--;
                                for(i=1;i<yyleng;i++) {
                                    if (    yytext[i]  == '\''
                                        && (i+1) < yyleng
                                        && yytext[i+1]== '\''
                                    ) i++ ;
                                    printf("%c",yytext[i]) ;
                                }
                                printf("\n");
```
Only part of this sample program is shown

1 Reference: Niklaus Wirth. PASCAL-S: a subset and its implementation.
Eidgenössische Technische Hochschule Zürich, Institut für Informatik.

have been re-compiled. Also, since each program can have a number of versions, the programmer sometimes becomes confused as to which versions should be used in the composite program.

It is difficult for a programmer himself to develop such a composite program that he can supervise himself, and even more difficult for another person to make that program. The program called **make** helps to ease this kind of difficulty.

In order to use **make**, a file which lists the operations to be performed (such as compiling) must be prepared. After a general outline is prepared, the work is then described in more detail. This file makes the files' relationship clear even to a person who is using the program for the first time. It is as if the writer of the program were writing detailed instructions for other users.

make causes the compiling to be performed exactly as instructed by this file, but without doing as wasteful a thing as re-compiling the entire composite program every time one of the component programs is altered. For example, as we explained once before, make compares the dates and times at which the source program and object program were created to determine which is newer. If the object program is newer then it can be used as is; if not, the program must be re-compiled.

Creation of Documents

ED

This is a conversational-type Line editor. It is the standard basic program used by UNIX to create and modify documents. There are two ways to specify a line, by a number which gives its place in order or by a pattern of characters which occurs on that line.

To save labor on the part of the person doing the editing, there are a number of abbreviated notations and symbols which have special meanings.

Using **ed**, it is possible to break files up, recombine the parts, and insert new or old parts relatively easily. The efficiency of editing is further improved by the capability to have the same processing performed on a number of lines.

During editing, it is possible to activate the shell in order to execute ordinary UNIX commands. There is also a capability to encode the contents of a file so that other people can't read it. Even the super user is not able to decode the contents of such a coded file. This encoding is done by a program called **crypt**.

SPELL

This program compares all of the words in a document file with the 25,000 entries in the UNIX dictionary, and any words that are not in the dictionary are displayed on the screen. This permits typographical errors to be discovered. Of course, just because a word is not in the dictionary does not automatically mean it is wrong, and, conversely, a spelling mistake might be missed if a word is misspelled so that it comes out being spelled like another word. Nevertheless, this capability succeeds in catching most spelling mistakes. At present, **spell** is only available the English language.

There are a number of different programs for UNIX

TYPO

This is another program used to catch typographical errors, but unlike **spell** it does not use a dictionary. It judges that a certain spelling is unlikely on a statistical basis, and the questionable word is displayed on the screen.

The use of both **spell** and **typo** results in a great reduction of spelling and typographical errors.

Formatting of Documents

TROFF and NROFF
These programs put documents into a good-looking format. By placing **troff/nroff** commands between sentences, the kind of type to be used for letters, whether lines are to be aligned on the right side and/or left side, indentation, titles and other features of a neat document format can be specified.

 troff prepares output for phototypesetters and **nroff** for printers.

 An inexperienced person would do well to use a standard package of formatting commands, which makes it possible to easily create documents in a standard format. Examples of such standard packages are **ms**, **me** and **man**.

EQN (equation)
This program is used to polish up the format of mathematical equations, which involve the use of special characters and symbols. The Greek letters and other special symbols are output for final specification by **troff**. Integrals, matrices, etc. can also be easily printed. Subscripts and superscripts are automatically reduced in size. There is another program called **checkeq** which checks **eqn** commands.

TBL (table)
This program is used to prepare tables which occur in a document. The kind of type to use can be specified, and framework lines can be drawn. Comparable digits of numbers can be aligned, and numbers aligned on either their right or left sides.

 The use of **troff** or **nroff**, **eqn** and **tbl** together makes it easy to format even the most complicated of documents.

REFER (reference)
Searching a bibliographic data base, this program automatically finds the references to the bibliography which contains keywords. This is very often used to prepare the bibliography of reference literature at the end of a book or technical paper. However, the data base of reference must be input to each system separately.

Processing of Files

There are many programs which are used for the processing of files. By combining these, even more complicated operations on files can be performed.

SORT
This program changes the order of lines in a file so that they are in a certain order, and outputs the result. The ordering is usually done in ascending order of the **ASCII** code, which is a most popular way to represent characters inside computers, but it can also be done in descending order. Other orders can also be specified as desired. This is one of the most commonly performed operations on files.

UNIQ (unique)
When two successive lines are identical, this program deletes one of them so that only one remains. This is often used in combination with **sort**.

TR (trans)
This program performs a translation on all specified characters that appear in a file. It is sometimes possible to save labor by using a special symbol and then converting it later to any of several characters. Another possibility is

"sort", "uniq", "tr" commands

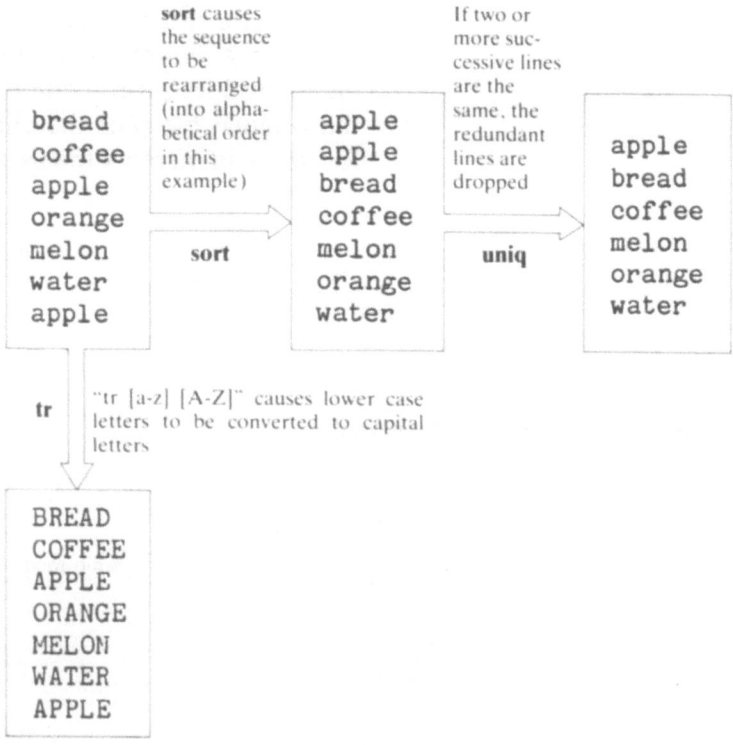

that all capital letters in a file could be converted to lower case letters.

However, conversion is only done on one letter at a time. Whole words, for example, cannot be converted.

DIFF (difference)
This program looks for the differences between two files. We have previously discussed the similar program **cmp** (compare), which tells only whether two files are identical or not; **diff** displays the differences.

In addition, since these differences can be expressed in "**ed**" command format, if only these differences are stored, one of the files together with the differences can be used to regenerate the other. We have previously looked at a situation in which this capability can be very convenient. For example, if certain changes are made in a file to produce several different versions of it, storing only the original file plus the changes usually requires much less space in memory than storing all of the complete files.

"diff" command   %cat food1

```
bread
coffee
apple
orange       File food1
melon
water
apple
```

%diff food1 food2 ← What is the difference between food1 and food2 ?

%cat food2

```
bread
tea
apple
orange
melon        File food2
coffee
sugar
water
apple
```

```
2c2
< coffee      On the second line one file
---           contains "coffee" while the
> tea         other contains "tea"
5a6,7
> coffee      File food2 has "coffee" and
> sugar       "sugar" below "melon"
```

%diff -e food1 food2 ← When you add the option "-e", you obtain a file such as the following

By storing this file, it becomes possible to reproduce "food2" from "food1" whenever desired, making it unnecessary to store "food2" in full

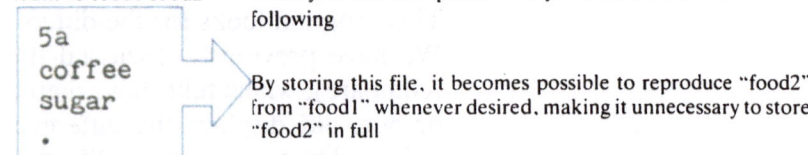

"comm" command

After file is operated on by **sort** and **uniq**

File food1	File food2
apple	apple
bread	bread
coffee	coffee
melon	melon
orange	orange
water	sugar
	tea
	water

Output of **comm**

Fistr file only	Second file only	Common elements
		apple
		bread
		coffee
		melon
		orange
	sugar	
	tea	
		water

COMM (common)

This program compares two files line by line and gives separate output of lines which are only in one file, lines which are only in the other file, and lines which are common to both files.

One possible application of this program is to prepare a list of people who belong to both of two different organizations. In such a case, the files must first be arranged lexicographically ascending order of the ASCII code by using **sort**.

GREP

This program outputs all lines from text files which contain a certain pattern of characters. It is also possible to output all lines which do not contain the pattern, to count the number of times the pattern appears and to output the numbers (in sequence) of the lines in which it appears. Two or more files can be searched at once. This is extremely useful for locating which files contain, for instance, references to a particular person, place or computer symbol.

SED (stream editor)

This is a non-conversational type of editor. It uses a file of instructions, and applies this file to the file which is to be modified. Control flows for selection, repetition, etc. can be given as commands, so fairly complicated processing can be performed.

AWK

This program searches for a certain specified pattern in a file and then performs some processing on it. We have already discussed the program **grep** which searches for a pattern, and the program **sed** which can perform processing on a file; **awk** combines them and also has additional functions to make it easier to use.

awk can use control flows and perform numerical calculations on files. It can also use variables. Since **awk** is not as complicated as a language such as C, it is relatively easy for beginners to use.

"grep" command

```
$ grep COMPLEX cpl.c
typedef struct {float re,im;} COMPLEX ;
         COMPLEX  z1,z2,z ;
COMPLEX  *z1, *z2, *p ;
COMPLEX  *z1, *z2, *q ;
COMPLEX  *z1, *z2, *p ;
```

This command might, for example, be used to extract all lines containing the character string "COMPLEX" from a very long program written in C (here called "cpl.c")

Example of an AWK program

```
#user login name table
#input data file is /etc/passwd.
#NR is a current line number.
BEGIN    { print "****** KUNII LAB. USER LOGIN NAME TABLE ******";
           FS =":"
         }
         {if (NR%3 == 1 || NR%3 == 2) { printf " %10d | %10s",NR,$1   }
                 else { printf  "%10d | %10s\n",NR,$1 }
         }
END      { print;
           print "total = ",  NR
         }
```

Games, CAI, Miscellaneous

The UNIX software provided by the Bell Telephone Laboratories includes a number of games. The user can play against the computer at games such as backgammon, chess, checkers, blackjack, mazes, etc. Since the software is good, the computer is a strong adversary and it is hard for the user to win.

One can also use UNIX for CAI (Computer Aided Instruction), for which there is a program called **learn**. **learn** is a program which a user uses to learn UNIX commands, sitting at a terminal solving the drill problems that UNIX gives him.

Since all of the UNIX command manuals are stored in an auxiliary storage device, they can be displayed on the terminal screen at any time. This eliminates the inconvenience of having to carry bulky manuals around. If the user momentarily forgets how to use the command on the computer, all he has to do is display the manual. When you create a new command, you should prepare its manual file too. Otherwise, other users cannot use it.

The manual can be displayed on the screen

This completes our discussion of the basic UNIX software. There is also additional software which the system supervisor uses for backup and maintenance.

There are also a number of graphic packages which are for use with the Tektronix 4014 graphic terminal.

CSHELL from UCB

The UCB version of UNIX has, in addition to the command interpreter shell, a second command interpreter called "cshell". Some users prefer this interpreter, and use it instead of shell. The choice is up to the user. The functions of cshell include the following (according to 4BSD):

· Job control function

cshell permits a background job to be temporarily stopped during execution, and started up again later; and a foreground job can be changed to a background job.

· Stacking of directories

cshell has a stack which permits a directory setting to be remembered. When a user transfers to an other directory, he pushes the current directory into the stack, and when he wants to return to the former directory, he can do it by specifying its number. This makes it easier to specify transfer between directories.

· History function

cshell has a history function, which stores the command lines which have been executed. Each line is numbered;

Example of history function

```
128  h
129  history
130  write shirota
131  jobs
132  mail
133  awk -f test.a /etc/passwd
134  history
135  awk -f test.a psswd
136  awk -f test.a passwd
137  history
138  vi temp
139  vi test.a
140  cat test.a
141  history
142  ls
143  ll
144  vi test.a
145  history
146  cat temp
147  man awk
148  q
149  history
150  grep comment test.a
151  history
152  history > temp
```

Example of a cshell procedure

```
#           birthday information
set dt = `date`
set month = $dt[2]
set day   = $dt[3]
while(1)
        set line = ($<)
        if ("$line" == "") break
        set line = ($line)
        if ("$month" == "$line[2]" && "$day" == "$line[3]") then
            echo '*******************************************'
            if ("$user" == "$line[1]") then
                    echo Happy birthday to you!
            else    echo Today is "$line[1]"\'s birthday!
            endif
            echo '*******************************************'
        endif
end
```

if that line number or part of the command name is specified, the command is executed again.

In addition, these commands can be modified before execution. Rather than key in all of a long complicated command two or more times when perhaps only one character is to be changed (perhaps to correct a spelling error), this function can be used to make the correction.
· Aliases

Command lines, including options and arguments, can be given aliases. Reducing a long command name to a short alias (for example, replacing "history" by "h") can save a great deal of work.

cshell is functionally similar to shell, but differs from it in also having the above functions and also certain other capabilities, such as added capabilities for handling variables and added control mechanisms (switch and foreach statements, etc.).

Additions to System III

The software described above is in Version 7 of UNIX. Each version of UNIX has slightly different software. The later the version, the more capabilities it provides; the capabilities of previous versions are nearly always retained. Most UNIX systems sold today are Version 7, although a few Version 6 systems are still in use.

A version called **UNIX The Programmer's Workbench** (abbreviated **PWB/UNIX**) has more software added, notably the programs called **rje** and **sccs**. The newest version, called **System III**, combines the software of Version 7 with that of PWB/UNIX, plus some additional software.

Since we have already described the software in Version 7, here we will only describe the principal additions to System III via PWB/UNIX.

RJE (remote job entry)
This program permits a computer on which UNIX runs to be connected to an IBM/360 or IBM/370 host computer. The smaller computer with UNIX can then be used to do work on the IBM computer. Work is sent from UNIX to the IBM computer, and the results are sent back. In other words the smaller computer with UNIX functions as a card reader and printer for the IBM computer.

SCCS (source code control system)
Even small changes in a source program can produce a number of versions. If all of these versions are stored, the file capacity can soon become saturated. It is at least partly for this reason that the **diff** command was created for use in editing. This makes it possible to store only one original program and the differences, and then regenerate the different versions as they are needed.

sccs is a greatly expanded version of **diff**. **sccs** not only stores the necessary information and regenerates the files, but also keeps track of when each version was created, by whom and for what purpose. This information is very useful for program maintenance.

In addition to the usual languages (C, Fortran), SNO-BOL is available on System III. SNOBOL is a widely used symbol processing language which is especially well suited for processing character strings.

The software described so far is all very basic software which has been developed in research institutions. There is a good deal of additional software on the market. Also, various companies sell versions of software which make it possible to use computer languages such as COBOL, BASIC, FORTRAN and PASCAL. One can expect that software companies will continue to put out a steady supply of new software for use with UNIX.

MISCELLANEOUS FEATURES

Fully Duplex Communications

Since a **full duplex system** is used for communications between a terminal and the main computer on which UNIX runs, communications from the terminal to the computer are completely separate from communications from the computer to the terminal.

This makes it possible to keep keying input in, without waiting for a response from the computer. Without this feature, a user who is a good typist cannot proceed at his own pace in keying in input; this feature makes UNIX easier to use than other systems which do not have it. In particular, during editing, prompts requesting the next input are not used by UNIX, so as not to interrupt the steady flow of input.

But if the input proceeds faster than the arrival of responses from UNIX, the two may be mixed on the display screen.

anger... frustration

Half-duplex

I wonder if any more data can squeeze in!

A full duplex system is sure convenient

UNIX

UNIX Runs on Even Relatively Small Computers

One of the main characteristics of UNIX is its simplicity. This makes it easy both to understand and to expand the system.

What can be called the heart of the UNIX system, the **kernel**, resides permanently in main memory. It performs jobs such as the following:

- Allocation of memory to the different processes

- Parallel processing under the time-sharing system

- Supervision of the file system

- Input/output to/from external memory devices and input/output devices

This kernel is compact, requiring only 60 to 80 kilobytes of memory. For this reason, the main memory capacity needed to run UNIX is relatively small, so that UNIX can be run on a fairly small computer. Bell Telephone Laboratories has supplied System III for use on the following computers. The main memory capacity needed to run System III is written after the name of each computer.

PDP-11/23	256 kilobytes
PDP-11/34	256 kilobytes
PDP-11/45	256 kilobytes
PDP-11/44	0.5–1 megabytes
PDP-11/70	0.5–1 megabytes
VAX-11/780	1–2 megabytes

Easily Transferred System

The ease with which UNIX can be transferred to new machines is one of the main reasons why it has come to be used on main frame computers and widely on 16-bit microcomputers. Since almost all of the UNIX system, including the kernel, is written in the C language, the system is easily expanded or transferred to a new machine. If the target machine has a C compiler, then UNIX C programs can be compiled and run on that machine. If all the work had to be done by an assembler, it would be troublesome. Because UNIX is written in the high-level language C, however, there is little dependence on the machine itself and these parts written in an assembler and C cannot be transferred.

Because it is so easily transferred to new machines, the use of UNIX on 16-bit and 32-bit microcomputers is expanding steadily. In the next few years, many more 32-bit microcomputers will be sold; many of these will have several tens of megabytes of internal memory, several hundred megabytes of external memory and chips which can do floating decimal point operations. In this situation, the ease of transferring UNIX to new machines is expected to be an important factor in making it widely used.

To use UNIX with new types of peripheral devices, it will be necessary to modify the kernel. Since the kernel is written in C, any necessary alterations should be easy to carry out.

In Conclusion

UNIX is a powerful operating system which has many high-level utility programs and is capable of running a number of jobs at once. It has many applications including office automation, network control and control of numerically controlled machinery. Since it also has superior capabilities as a program development system, UNIX should become even more widely used in the future. UNIX provides a better programming environment for its many users.

Authors' Postscript

Did reading this book help you to understand UNIX? If so, we will be very happy. We tried our best to develop the text and examples to fill the requirements of executives to lead corporate strategies and planning for software development. It was a pleasant and enlighting job for us to do this with constant interaction with our friends who are company executives.

As we wrote this book we came to feel like we would like to start using UNIX ourselves. The good people at Chuo Electronics Co., Ltd. gave us the chance to do so on their CEC8000 computer. We want to thank them for doing so and also for helping us obtain information about UNIX.

While writing this book, the following people helped us a great deal: the University of Tokyo Research Associate Kazunori Yamaguchi, and Atsushi Iizawa and Katsumi Kanasaki of Ricoh Company, Ltd.

It is impossible to list all of the other people who have helped us in the course of writing this book, but we want to thank them all for their assistance. The critical comments by Associate Professor Kigen Hasebe of University of Library and Information Science and graduate student Jun Murai of Keio University on some ambiguous statements in the first Japanese edition greatly assisted the authors' effort to make the sentences easier to understand.

We hope that you will find this book useful as you start to look into for developing corporate plans for software.

Yukari Shirota
Tosiyasu L. Kunii

References

Bourne SR (1982) The UNIX system. Addison-Wesley, Massachusetts

Christian K (1983) The UNIX operating system. John Wiley & Sons, New York

Comer D (1984) Operating system design — the XINU approach. Prentice-Hall, New Jersey

Dolotta TA, Haight RC (1977) PWB/UNIX overview and synopsis of facilities. Bell Laboratories, New Jersey

Dolotta TA, Haight RC, Mashey JR (1978) UNIX time-sharing system: the programmer's workbench. Bell System Technical Journal 57: 2177–2200

Gauthier RL (1981) Using the UNIX system. Prentice-Hall, Reston, Virginia

Hwang K, Wah BW, Briggs FA (1981) Engineering computer network (ECN): a hard-wired network of UNIX computer systems. In: AFIPS, National Computer Conference, vol 50. AFIPS Press, Arlington, Virginia

Ishida H (1983) UNIX (in Japanese). Kyoritsu Shuppan, Tokyo

Johnson SC, Ritchie DM (1978) Unix time-sharing system. Bell System Technical Journal 57: 2021–2048

Kernighan BW, Pike P (1984) The UNIX programming environment. Prentice-Hall, New Jersey

Kernighan BW, Ritchie DM (1978) The C programming language. Prentice-Hall, New Jersey

Mason J, Shaw G (1981) Implementing ethernet from soup to nuts. Data Communications, December: 74–80

Meijer A, Peeters P (1981) Computer network architectures. Pitman Books, London

Naemura K, Tabata K, Asano S (1980) Computer network technology (in Japanese). Information Processing Society, Tokyo

Plum T (1983) Learning to program in C. Prentice-Hall, New Jersey

Programmer's manual for UNIX system III, vols 2A, 2B (1981) Western Electric Company, North Carolina

Saito N, Takeichi M, Ishihata K (1982) C — language and programming (in Japanese). Sangyo Tosho, Tokyo

Silvester PP (1984) The UNIX system guidebook. Springer-Verlag, New York

Sobell MG (1984) A practical guide to the UNIX system. The Benjamin/Cummings Publishing, Menlo Park, California

Tanenbaum AS (1981) Network protocols. In: ACM Computer Surveys, vol 13. Association for Computing Machinery, New York

The UNIX system encyclopedia (1984) Yates Ventures, Los Altos, California

Thomas R, Yates J (1982) A user guide to the UNIX system. McGraw-Hill, Berkeley, California

UNIX programmer's manual, vol 2C (1983) Department of Electrical Engineering and Computer Science, University of California, Berkeley, California

UNIX time-sharing system: UNIX programmer's manual, revised and expanded version (1983) Bell Laboratories (ed) Halt, Rinehart and Winston, New York

UNIX time-sharing system: UNIX programmer's manual, seventh edition, vols 1, 2A, 2B (1979) Bell Laboratories, New Jersey

J. Encarnação, E. G. Schlechtendahl

Computer Aided Design

Fundamentals and System Architectures

1983. 176 figures (12 of them in color). IX, 346 pages
(Symbolic Computation, Computer Graphics)
ISBN 3-540-11526-9

The book is a thorough introduction to the fundamentals of Computer Aided Design (CAD). Both Computer Science and Engineering Sciences contribute to the particular flavor of CAD. Design is interpreted as an iterative process involving specification, synthesis, analysis, and evaluation, with CAD as a tool to provide computer assistance in all these phases.
The major issues treated in the book are: System architecture; components and interfaces; data base aspects in CAD; man-machine communication; computer graphics for geometrical design; drafting and data representation; the interrelationship between CAD and numerical methods; and simulation, and optimization. Economic, ergonomic, and social aspects are considered as well.

G. Enderle, K. Kansy, G. Pfaff

Computer Graphics Programming

GKS – The Graphics Standard

1984. 93 figures, some in color. XVI, 542 pages
(Symbolic Computation, Computer Graphics)
ISBN 3-540-11525-0

The book covers computer graphics programming on the base of the Graphical Kernel System, GKS. GKS is the first international standard for the functions of a computer graphics system. It offers capabilities for creation and representation of two-dimensional pictures, handling input from graphical workstations, structuring and manipulating pictures, and for storing and retrieving them. It represents a methodological framework for the concepts of computer graphics and establishes a common understanding for computer graphics systems, methods and applications. This book gives an overview over the GKS concepts, the history of the GKS design and the various system interfaces. A significant part of the book is devoted to a detailed description of the application of GKS functions both in a Pascal and a FORTRAN-language environment.

Springer-Verlag
Berlin
Heidelberg
New York
Tokyo

R. Gleaves

Modula-2 for Pascal Programmers

1984. 18 figures. X, 145 pages. (Springer Books on Professional
Computing). ISBN 3-540-96051-1

Contents: New Concepts. – Differences from Pascal. – Utility
Modules. – Appendix 1: Glossary. – Appendix 2: Syntax Diagrams. –
Appendix 3: Reserved Words and Symbols. – Appendix 4: Standard
Identifiers. – Appendix 5: ASCII Character Set. – Index.

Modula-2 is a modern systems programming language which offers
significant improvements over its predecessor Pascal. "Modula-2 for
Pascal Programmers" builds upon the Pascal programmer's
knoweldge by focusing on differences from Pascal, and by introduc-
ing concepts unique to Modula-2. A major strength of the book lies in
its practical approach: Numerous example programs are provided,
many of which emphasize basic Modula-2-programming facilities.
The book also includes syntax diagrams and a glossary of Modula-2
terminology.

N. Wirth

Programming in Modula-2

2nd, corrected edition. 1983. IV, 176 pages. (Texts and Monographs
in Computer Science). ISBN 3-540-12206-0
(1st edition "Wirth, Programming in Modula-2", 1982)

Contents: Part 1: Introduction. A first example. A notation to
describe syntax. Representation of Modula programs. Statements and
expressions. Control structures. Elementary data types. Constant and
variable declarations. The data structure Array. – Part 2: Procedures.
The concept of locality. Parameters. Function procedures. Recursion.
– Part 3: Type declarations. Enumeration types. Subrange types. Set
types. Record types. Records with variant parts. Dynamic structures
and pointers. Procedure types. – Part 4: Modules. Definition and
implementation parts. Program decomposition into modules. Local
modules. Sequential input and output. Screen-oriented input and
output. – Part 5: Low-level facilities. Concurrent processes and
coroutines. Device handling, concurrency, and interrupts. – Report
on the Programming Language Modula-2. – Appendix 1: The Syntax
of Modula-2. – Appendix 2: The ASCII character set. – Index.

Springer-Verlag
Berlin
Heidelberg
New York
Tokyo